This Book Belongs To

Dianne T. Little

IN TUNE WITH HEAVEN

IN TUNE WITH HEAVEN

VANCE HAVNER

Foreword by Billy Graham

BAKER BOOK HOUSE
Grand Rapids, Michigan 49516

ISBN: 0-8010-4335-2

Printed in the United States of America

Contents

Foreword

I remember that when I was a teenager my mother would always read Vance Havner in the *Charlotte Observer.* It was one of the inspirations of my teenage life.

Now his wit, metaphor, simile, vivid description, and humor have all been combined in this book.

He was pastor of some of the South's largest churches. He was probably the most sought-after speaker and Bible teacher in the country for a number of years. All the great Bible conferences and conventions wanted him. The crowds came by the thousands to hear him. Many years ago he was sometimes called the "Will Rogers" of the American pulpit.

He was a unique preacher and observer of the passing scene of the twentieth century. I knew him since 1936 and had the privilege of preaching his funeral.

This collection is just as refreshing as some of his preaching, teaching, and columns were more than fifty years ago. Once you begin reading it, you will find it very difficult to put down.

May God use this book to bless you, inspire you, convict you, and, yes, give hours of amusement.

Billy Graham

Introduction

In the fall of 1926, Vance Havner wrote several letters to "The Open Forum," the editor's pad for expression of views by the people who read the *Charlotte Observer.* The editor, impressed by this twenty-five-year-old man's style of writing, as well as the positive response from readers, requested that Vance Havner write a weekly column for this daily newspaper. The series of columns, titled "Havner's Reflections" began on November 28, 1926, and continued through the late '30s, appearing in each Sunday's edition.

Until his death in 1986, Vance Havner continued to write. While proclaiming the Word of God through his pulpit ministry, leading untold numbers to Christ and to a deeper spiritual dedication, he also wrote thirty-eight books. These books, along with other writings have brought encouragement, guidance, and blessing to thousands.

Vance Havner willed his estate and writings to The Vance H. Havner Scholarship Fund, an organization established in 1978 by some Greensboro, North Carolina, businessmen for the purpose of providing financial aid to students preparing for full-time Christian vocations. The Board of Directors of this organization felt that modern readers would find Havner's columns, now more than a half-century old, amazingly relevant to contemporary society. All royalties from Havner's writings as well as contributions to the scholarship fund are entirely invested in student scholarships. Contributions or requests for information may be addressed to: The Vance H. Havner Scholarship Fund, Inc., P.O. Box 1048, Greensboro, North Carolina 27402.

PART 1

Spirituality—
In Tune with Heaven

1

Are You Tuned In?

I sit in my home each evening and hear music from afar brought to me out of the air by that strange little device, the radio. Nearby lives my neighbor. The same music is all around him just as strong and beautiful but he does not hear it. He has no radio and is not tuned in.

I have found now and then in my little career a few fine souls who manage to live in touch with a world far greater than this small range of stock markets, politics, and country clubs. They seem to hear music and to see vistas that the rest of us somehow miss. They live among their neighbors, in the world but not of it, outwardly working like all the rest with things temporal but inwardly drinking of springs eternal.

Somehow they are different. And I think the difference is this: With most of us the temporal is our home and the spiritual is only accidental and incidental; with these finer souls the situation is reversed; they live in the spiritual while the temporal is incidental. With us the material world is an end in itself; with them the material is only a means to a spiritual end.

Some people live in tune with heaven. I have noticed that those who do are not smarter than the rest of folks; they are not in better circumstances nor more educated nor more skillful in things spiritual. There is no favoritism here. We have a habit of thinking, "Ah, that is well enough for people who have time for such things, for preachers and old ladies and poets. But no one with dyspepsia or poverty or a mother-in-law such as I have, has time for such Pollyanna sentiments." But I have observed that those who live in tune with the infinite are often as poor and as unfortunate and have as un-ideal surroundings as the rest of us. Externalities have nothing to do with it, it lies deeper than that.

Just as a man with a radio hears from a world that those about him without radios are strangers to, just so do some live among us, working as we work and outwardly one of us, but inwardly in connection with spheres far greater than the world of radio. They move through this complex and befuddled age not depending as we do upon money and position and pleasure for their lives. While we rave about baseball and stocks and dividends and politics, they casually mention such things but it is evident to us that their thoughts are really upon things higher. We may pass them up as strange; we cannot talk their language; but in our best moments we suspect that although they may be very plain and common and dwell in a cottage whilst we stay in mansions—we suspect that they perhaps have the best of it after all, and that it is we who hold the sack!

To thus live in tune with the eternal may not interest us, but it is the only achievement of life worth knowing. It is the object of religion and the goal of existence. It is what we are here for:

> There are in the loud, storming tide
> Of this world's care and crime
> With whom the melodies abide
> Of the everlasting chime;
> Who carry music in their heart
> Through dusky lane and wrangling mart;
> Who ply their daily task with busier feet
> Because their secret souls a holier strain repeat.

They live in tune with the infinite. Do you?

February 23, 1930

2
Strength Through Weakness

Most people fortify themselves from without. They gather unto themselves fame and finery, property and publicity; they build a little bulwark of stocks and bonds, mansions and money, cars and collateral—and imagine themselves secure. The world has gone wild over this outside line of defense; in its eyes a man has made himself safe when he has landed a big job, cleaned up on the stock market, or learned how to pull wires to his own advantage.

The trouble with this kind of stability is, it isn't stable. A little shift of circumstance may blow away our puny arrangements and land us in despair. And even if nothing happens to one's external fortunes, if they are all he has, his worst enemy is inside his fortress, not outside.

Often it does a man good to lose every outside prop and dependence. If he has depended upon them for his safety and happiness it is an awful wrench, but when the smoke of his disaster has cleared away he can come out of it far richer than when he went in.

It is a fine thing when a man learns that his real resources are within, that if his spirit be strong and his soul wellknit, nothing that happens from without can subdue him. Such a man as that knows how to value properly money and possessions and prestige. He does not despise them but he knows they are incidental and does not depend upon them for his security or happiness. If he have them, well and good; if he lose them, he is not destitute—his real resources are untouched.

Some people, happily learn this without the help of dire misfortune; but if one needs be reduced to beggary to find it out, the price is not too great.

Paul said, "When I am weak, then am I strong" (2 Cor. 12:10). He had none of these external resources; he was poor, despised, homeless, persecuted. He was conscious of inner frailties and personal weaknesses that distressed him. But he turned it into a blessing, for his own poverty drove him to count earthly treasures nothing and lean the more heavily upon the eternal. His own weakness was his strength.

Indeed, he speaks of God saying to him, "My strength is made perfect in weakness." The world today would have us glorify our own selves, our personal smartness and cleverness. Religion would make a man conscious of his own frailty and dependent utterly upon God, counting himself only a medium through which the infinite may work.

Such an idea is not palatable to some psychologists and modern humanists. But deeper minds perceive its truth as did William James when he says:

> There is a state of mind known to religious men, but to no others, in which the will to assert ourselves and hold our own has been displaced by a willingness to close our mouths and be as nothing in the floods and waterspouts of God.

In this state of mind, he adds,

> The time for tension in our soul is over and that of happy relaxation, of calm deep breathing, of an eternal present with no discordant future to be anxious about, has arrived.

How far ahead of modern egotism is the happy state of those whose strength is from above, whose treasures are kept "where neither moth nor rust doth corrupt and where thieves do not break through nor steal" (Matt. 6:20).

May 25, 1930

3

Can You Stand Alone?

It is a gregarious age. Men run in droves. Yet, strangely enough, individuality is glorified. Educators have emphasized that each child is a world in himself, and must not be run through a common mold. But never has there been a generation more unanimously and monotonously alike. Modern mortals have about as much individuality as eggs in a basket.

We feel the blight of uniformity everywhere. A stereotyped and standardized race has reaped a harvest of dead and insipid sameness. Our dearth of national leadership tells a tale of many second-class politicians with no man who stands above the rest in the integrity of a peculiar and rugged distinctness. Our leaders are but instruments of cliques and clans. Where is one who can stand alone?

In the religious world there is a famine of spiritual giants. There are many fine men, but where is the prophet in the wilderness who rises above party to challenge men with "Thus saith the Lord"? We have become part of a vast and complicated system and we utter its voice and champion its policies. Even the ministry has become too much a regulated arrangement of promotions where loyalty to one sort of hierarchy or another is indispensable to success, and where to be different often brings the anathema of the higherups.

Bible preachers learned early the lesson of standing alone. Enoch and Noah in a corrupt generation; Moses amidst a grumbling people; Elijah, as rugged as his mountain retreats; Isaiah and Jeremiah in a decadent nation; Amos, the country preacher who "scandalized" the king's chapel and court by his flaming messages of judgment; Daniel in a foreign land; John the Baptist, the lone prophet of a religious but unspiritual day; Paul, the "fool for Christ's sake," the homeless trailblazer of the gospel. These belonged to no category, fitted into no established order; they were God's odd numbers.

It is not easy so to live. It is dangerous and risky and it is easy to be led into it to please one's own peculiar whims, rather than for Christ's sake. The principle of it has been used to cover the asininities of more fools than has any other argument. It has been the stock defense of mere sensationalists and cranks until the real virtue of it has come into disrepute.

For all that, the gregarious mood of the present age calls loudly for Christians who can stand alone. Too many ride the bandwagon of public sentiment. Too many are in the basement telling jokes at banquets and not enough are on the watchtower telling what of the night. The same condition that has made our national leaders of one stature threatens the church. We spend all our time building fences because we have so few who can fly.

Paul speaks of those who were "somewhat in conference." Being somewhat in conference becomes too easily an ideal. It is still well to heed the Lord's viewpoint about loving the chief seats in synagogues and to be called *rabbi*.

The high altitudes are still uncrowded. Diplomacy, tact, and cleverness, the ability to fall in with trends and capitalize situations—these sometimes rate more highly with us than loyalty to God. It is still costly to be faithful to the heavenly vision. He who so aspires had better discipline his soul for solitude.

June 25, 1933

4

A Little Path to Peace

For years I have watched the frantic search of men for the road to inward rest and peace. Philosophers seek it in books, wise men in mysteries, worldly folk in pleasure, the curious look for it in fads, church people in dogma and ritual. And most of us miss it by many miles.

Then I have observed a strange thing. The secret of peace belongs to a comparative few—many of them children, sick folk, humble and simple souls—the very sort we should think least qualified to find it. While the smart and sophisticated blunder along, looking for it up in the clouds, commoner souls find it early in the dust at their feet.

It is so simple the worldly wise pass it looking for the complex and elaborate—so humble the proud will not condescend to accept it. True, some brilliant and great ones reach it now and then, but they do so by divesting themselves of all their vaunted wisdom and returning to the second childhood of the spirit. It is the way of the childlike for unless "ye . . . become as little children, ye shall not enter the kingdom of heaven" (Matt. 18:3). The wise and prudent miss it, while it is revealed unto babes.

We have a mistaken notion nowadays that the smarter a man is, the better may he live. As a matter of fact, the humbler and simpler he is, the better chance he has of finding the little path to peace. The really great things of life are known by the simple.

Some will say: "You discourage investigation and soul struggles. This simple trust you advocate is the weak gesture of those simpletons who have not the brains nor the energy to reason things out, and so they sweetly trust to avoid the hard work of facing life and thinking it through."

But no one can think life through. Life is not a hard wall that you butt down with your head. Heart first—not head first—is the way through. These skeptical ones who set out to reason it out end up in despair or come back after all to the simple faith of a child. So, start with this humble trust and let it keep your heart at rest, while your head wrestles with this problem and that. Those who do so know that the wiseacres will come back to it anyway or be lost in the wilderness, so the humble start out with it instead of trying to think through to it.

The supreme secret of life does not belong to the superior heads and the mighty of earth. The salt of the earth is made of those common folk who have little enough sense to believe there is a God and to depend upon Him. They do not argue; they *know*. While professors and philosophers move heaven and earth trying to prove God in advance, these simple saints accept Him in advance and prove Him daily as they go. While the shrewd and the sophisticated groan along under innumerable burdens, these "ignorant" souls are relieved of life's strain and tension by leaving their burden with the Lord. And why not leave it all with the Lord? It is with Him anyway. All of our fretting cannot take it out of His hands. We are straining under a load that isn't there!

Look for the little path to peace. It does not lie along the highways of the wise nor the boulevards of the prudent. "God hath chosen the foolish . . . to confound the wise; . . . the weak . . . to confound the . . . mighty; And base things of the world, and . . . despised . . . and things which are not, to bring to naught things that are: That no flesh should glory in his presence (1 Cor. 1:27–29).

It is only a little path and easily missed by those who look for white ways.

January 26, 1929

5

The Master's Image

Miss Bessie cherished one regret throughout her life.

She was a very busy woman. Her husband had died, leaving her with four little children to feed and clothe. That sent her to the factory with its dust and smoke and grinding hours of weary toil. Each evening, when the whistle blew and she passed out the big iron gate, she had to hurry to the little yellow cottage down at the end of the dingy street, where the last electric light grows dim. Then she must cook and sew and put the children to bed with a prayer and a story.

Years passed, and the children married, and Miss Bessie found it easier. But somehow the feverish spirit of the mill had saturated her life, and she kept right on her busy way, even after she went to live with the youngest daughter in the city. There was plenty there for kind hearts and loving hands, and Miss Bessie reveled in it—carrying baskets of food to the O'Flahertys down the street when they were all laid up with flu and nobody to work; making little gingham dresses for Molly Anderson's baby, whose mother would never walk again; fixing up flowers for the sickroom where little Tommy Barstow lay twisted with paralysis; telling stories to the kiddies at the orthopedic hospital; carrying rag dolls to the tenement waifs; trying to keep old Grandpa Scroggins's gouty foot from hurting him any more than possible; and sitting up with Grandma Halsey while the family slept a bit. Miss Bessie didn't do it because she was overreligious nor was she trying to be a grownup Pollyanna. She simply loved it and thought nothing of reward.

But Miss Bessie always said: "I wish I had time to study the Bible and be a good Christian. The Good Book tells about letting the image of the Master be formed in you, and I'm afraid I'm so busy I don't stay with Him long enough to be much like Him. Someday I want to have time to meditate and pray and read about Jesus and try to be more like Him."

One day Miss Besssie fell sick, and the shadows gathered fast around her. And as she sat one evening on the broad, front porch and felt more keenly than ever her old regret, she dreamed a dream.

She dreamed that she stood with the Master and somehow she was not afraid. And before them as they stood passed a curious and motley procession: the O'Flahertys with their baskets, Molly Anderson and her baby, little Tommy Barstow with a bunch of flowers, the children in the orthopedic, the tenement kiddies with their rag dolls, old Grandpa Scroggins with his gouty foot, and Grandma Halsey in her chair. And behind these she beheld a fair saint with a face that shone as an angel's.

"Who is she?" Miss Bessie inquired of the Master.

"She is thyself," He softly replied.

"Myself!" Miss Bessie was astounded. "But I never had time to read and do much praying, and I never took time to be a saint. How can it be myself who spent so little time with Thee?"

And as she spoke the procession stopped, and the Master turned to Miss Bessie and said:

"I am not, dear woman, whom you think. I am the O'Flahertys; I am Molly Anderson before me. I am no dazzling god, satisfied with long prayers and hymns and litanies. It is not in dusty libraries and gilded sanctuaries that men find Me best. Do you know who I am? I am the O'Flahertys; I am Molly Anderson's baby; I am little Tommy Barstow and the tenement waifs; I am old Grandpa Scroggins and Grandma Halsey. And inasmuch as you did it unto one of the least of these you did it unto Me."

The procession moved on and Miss Bessie watched the beautiful saint who walked behind it—and as she looked she beheld the image of the Master in her face.

June 5, 1927

6

A Statement of Faith

I have no elaborate creed nor profound theology. I am only a rustic disciple of the Master, seeking in this complex modern age to regain something of the accents, the fragrance and color of old Galilee.

Years ago, a bewildered country boy, I decided to stake everything upon Jesus and His claim to be the answer of life. I have not run back every few days to do that over, for I meant it the first time and once is enough.

There are many matters connected with Jesus that I do not understand. I am not saved by understanding Jesus but by trusting Him. I do not understand all that He is but whatever He really is I accept. He claimed to be the truth about God and life and the answer to our needs. I have taken Him at His Word and am depending upon Him.

I cannot comprehend life. Most of it is beyond me, but I am not worrying about it. I try to live up to the little I know. If the way I live were even wrong, I would be right in living up to the best I know. And if there were no God and life were in charge of a satanic principle, I still would try to be good and take the consequences. Jesus is the best I know. Anyway you look at it, I am right in following Him.

I am in this world, and although I didn't ask to come, I'm rather glad I'm here. It is a complicated mixture of sunlight and shadow but it is a fine place for a game spirit, and I intend to live as though God were real and Jesus were His true interpretation. There are a lot of baffling puzzles that rise up when I strike out that road but not half so many as when I start out any other. I have to try some trail so why not the best I know?

The longer I live this way the more I am convinced that it is right. The evidence is cumulative; it grows as I go.

I am taking one day at a time. The commonplace hour is as important in the eternal values as my most thrilling moment. Whatever life means depends on how I look at it. The kingdom of heaven—or hell—is within me. I can make it a dull, stupid, monotony or a daring adventure.

I have learned that most of our fevers and fears are silly and not worth the trouble. And most of our miseries grow laughable in retrospect. I shall trust God as a child—it is the most reasonable attitude and produces best results. I try to do a little good, to keep in touch with life's better things, to divide and thus multiply my blessings. I have learned that to play is religion too, as well as to pray, and a laugh may be as holy as a liturgy.

I stay outdoors a good deal. Out there the dust blows out of the soul, the friction and tension of living are eased, and things assume their proper size and value in a saner perspective. Most of our miseries are born indoors. A quiet day along the river or a camp in the woods is the death of bugaboos.

I am just a leisurely rambler, not out to get rich or famous, taking time to pluck a blossom, listen to a bird song, watch the sun go down. Life is good when lived in simple faith that trusts and obeys.

And eventually I plan to cross the skyline and wander through new fields and finer sights in other lands.

It is an interesting world. The bitterness and pain drive weak souls to despair but to him who likes a risky venture the hardship only adds a challenge to the soul. Who wants a soft, harmless world? There is just enough acid with the sweet to give it tang, otherwise we should have a sickly, saccharine existence with dyspepsia of the soul.

August 10, 1930

7

Spiritual Luxuries

They may not admit it, but practically everybody in America is living and working for more luxuries.

The van Snoodles on Fifth Avenue are planning a more elaborate yacht; the O'Laffertys down in the tenements are figuring on a phonograph; and Farmer Perkins is calculating on buying a brand-new flivver. And so on we go, everybody from Julia O'Grady to the colonel's lady, saving and scrimping and skinning our neighbors so we can have luxuries. The ideal of the average man, no matter how he may sing at church "Lord, I care not for riches, neither silver nor gold," is to own a country villa and be a retired "villain" with a Pierce-Arrow in the carport and a butler who can keep his mouth shut in seven languages.

And why are we thus constituted, may I ask? Because, my dear, although this old mundane sphere has revolved for unnumbered centuries, and Chautauqua orators make good sums declaiming about progress, we still are in the Nut Age and we think, for all our religion, that the supreme object of life is to collect *things*. Although the richest character who ever trod these rugged trails declared that a man's life consists not in the abundance of things he possesses, we do not believe it. We pay preachers to preach about it but we do not believe it. For all our idealism, we are all out collecting for our curiosity shops, and the successful man is he who has scraped together in his junk heap the biggest assortment of furniture, gas buggies, crockery, frockery, and other garbage.

And yet for all I've said, the principle of living for luxuries is all right, it's in the workin's of it that we fall down. It is right to live for luxuries but we live for the wrong kind. For every material luxury there is a spiritual counterpart, and we miss it by living for tangible trifles instead of spiritual riches. Consider money. Money represents all luxuries, and it is for money that we live. If we do not live for money itself—we live for what it can buy. Well, suppose we swap luxuries, suppose we turn our money into better luxuries than cars and clothes, suppose we exchange these things for the finer luxuries of the mind and heart and soul. Instead of gathering to ourselves *things*, let us see how many good deeds, great thoughts, worthy achievements, we can lay up in the storehouse of our lives. That is what the Master meant by "laying up treasure in heaven." He was advising us to change our idea of what wealth meant, and to move up from living for goods to living for God. The world does not need to quit trying to get rich. That is a worthy ambition. The world simply needs to change its idea of what it means to be rich. When men learn that the only true wealth is spiritual, we will still have our rich men, but they will not be rated by how they stand in Wall Street.

I have but little of this world's wealth but I am rich. Others may dabble in stocks and bonds, but I can commune in my mind with the great souls of time, and that is a luxury. Some may dance the winter away at Palm Beach, but I can tramp the hills and dance in the woods to the orchestra of Nature, and that is a luxury. There are those who recline on soft cushions and dress in rich robes and wear diamonds. What are cushions but junk; what are dresses but rags; what are diamonds but stones? Others may claim the titles of royalty. *I* am a child of God. Others may be heirs to passing fortunes, *I* am heir to the universe. And so is any man who belongs to the spiritual aristocracy.

February 27, 1927

8

Spiritual Health

In this day when doctors and clinics cover the country as the waters cover the sea, it would be a good thing if, with our strides toward physical health, we took at least equal steps toward the health of the soul.

The spirit is supposed to be more important than the body, but from the little time we spend keeping it in good condition most of us do not seem to think so.

We need some clinics for sick souls. For back of all our other troubles, whether personal, social, financial, industrial, international or what not—yes, even back of all our bad health—lie our diseased souls. If our spirits were robust and vigorous, the rest of our ailments would automatically heal themselves.

The analogy between physical and spiritual health is perfect. In the natural and spiritual worlds the same principles exist.

The soul becomes diseased like the body. There are perhaps as many diseases. There are, for instance, such ailments as fever, poisoning, anemia, paralysis of the soul. There is pain and decay and atrophy and death of the inner man. There are stimulants and opiates that dull and deaden the soul and do more harm than good. And there are quack doctors and patent medicines and fake nostrums for the soul.

There is one specialist of the soul who has never lost a case. He enjoyed perfect spiritual health while here and imparted it to others, not by formulas but by simple faith. He has thousands of practitioners under Him who cannot cure by themselves any more than an M.D. can cure us. They only point to the Great Physician, just as the good doctor adjusts us with Nature. None of us enjoy perfect spiritual health anymore than we do physical, but we can have such an abundance of it as to be immune to spiritual pestilence and vigorously active and happy.

Religion, like medicine, is curative and preventative. Perhaps we have talked too much of its curative side. It does cure the diseased soul and innumerable are the testimonials from those who once were blind and now see. But better than that, its chief mission is to keep us from becoming sick. It charges the soul with a spiritual secretion that keeps it in health and destroys the germs and toxins of evil before they can fester and poison the heart. And religion, by making us spiritually strong, indirectly produces physical health as well.

There is surgery in the sanitorium of the soul. As with the body, drastic measures must be taken with the spirit. As the Great Specialist said the right eye or hand must be removed—that is, any hindrance to spiritual health must be amputated even though it leaves the patient maimed. Spiritual invalids cannot eat strong meat and must deny themselves pleasures that normal souls can enjoy. Spiritual health is also built up gradually and slowly, not all at once. It is cumulative and must grow by discipline. We develop health of the soul as of the body by daily programs of rest, diet, exercise. And happy is the man who has gained vigor of soul and can go about helping the soul-sick of earth to the health he enjoys. It is great to be a doctor of souls.

And health of the spirit is like health of the body, not so much a matter of formulas and prescriptions and ologies, as it is a matter of living simply and beautifully in harmony with the laws of the spiritual world. The secret of soul health is not put up in the laboratories of private theologians. It is in simple adherence to the great fundamentals.

Best of all, the healthy soul never dies.

May 20, 1928

9

Keep Wondering

A normal child is fresh and full of wonder at the world around him. He has not lived long enough to be accustomed to everything, so he moves in continuous expectancy. Of course even children are becoming so hard-boiled in these sophisticated times that this does not always apply. I am speaking of normal children, who are as God meant them to be.

Now a Christian must be childlike (see Matt. 18:3), and one mark of a childlike (not childish!) Christian is a constant sense of wonder. The world around us has lost that, even in the natural realm, and has become cynical, nonchalant, and cold. Our critical faculty is overdeveloped at the expense of our appreciation and sympathy. We are so afraid that somebody will "put something over on us" that we live with fingers crossed and take everything we hear with a grain of salt. We have been "taken in" and double-crossed until we have built up a defense wall but, alas, in doing so we have imprisoned ourselves in a cynicism and disillusionment that is worse than what we are trying to guard against! We are so afraid of being gullible that we are the most gullible generation up to now. We fall for more fads and isms and gold bricks and cure-alls than any race that ever lived.

Someone has said that men used to believe everything and now they believe nothing. This attitude has crept into church. We Christians have been deceived by people until we tend to become dubious of everything that savors of the unusual. If a brother claims healing, we assume a questioning air, and look very incredulous. If a sister claims a mighty experience of the Spirit, we immediately are on our guard against extravagance. Now, granted that much error is going the rounds, and that we cannot swallow all the colorful stories we hear, yet we must beware of that more dangerous evil of losing our sense of openness to the miraculous and the marvelous. It is better to have loved and lost than never to have loved, and it is better to believe too much and be disappointed than forever doubt. "Love believeth all things" and while that does not mean a

gullible credulity for everything that comes along, it does mean a childlike sense of wonder toward a God who is ever doing wonders.

Today we credit anything that happens to any cause rather than the supernatural. If someone is healed, we admit any cause than the direct operation of God. If someone is possessed of great power, we find ourselves ascribing it to personality, magnetism—anything but the Holy Spirit. We have heard so many claim these things—and then later prove to be untrustworthy—that we have become disillusioned and cynical. Sometimes older Christians who have known many who professed these things become rather hard in later years, when so many show up badly after having begun such a good profession.

God help us to keep our childlike sense of wonder. May we rise every morning wondering what God will do today. Let us go to His house saying, "I wonder what will take place today?" If someone claims a glorious blessing, let us believe the best until we have to believe something else—if ever we do. For otherwise we are surely building up a poisonous thought habit and attitude of incredulity and doubt that will leave us as hard as the Pharisees of old.

February 21, 1937

31

10

Broadcasting God

I walk down the streets of a little town. Almost every house has a radio, and every one seems to be going. The president of the United States is speaking. I pass by a palatial residence, and from it comes his voice through a costly set. Along by more modest houses, and still the same voice from cheaper loud speakers. Then along the poor folk's row, and yet the chief executive's voice sounds out through plain rooms and out broken windows to me. All sorts of homes but the voice is the same! Radio outfits of varied makes and values but the message is one!

Life is like that. I like to think that, no matter what street we live on, what price our house, we are as near God as anybody else. The same voice that one hears from the mansion by radio is all around the cheapest house in town waiting to be received and expressed. God is no respecter of persons. He is as near the back alley as the boulevard, and wherever a humble heart will accept and transmit His message He will speak. The eternal voice will come into your modest little dwelling, your simple heart, as gladly as into the cultured, prosperous folk on Main Street. They have no monopoly on God. They may have the edge on you in money, finery, furnishings, but as the same programs come through cheap sets as through exquisite cabinets, so the heavenly music will come to your house no matter where you live. "The word is nigh thee, even in thy mouth, and in thy heart."

What a fine world if we could walk along by every home and from every human heart the Chief Magistrate of the Universe were speaking! Is God broadcasting from your house? Alas, there is jazz and gossip and business and stock-market reports and profanity and falsehood. For most lives are not tuned in on God. And even on Sundays, if the sermon grows too long they switch off to some more congenial theme. When the orchestra of heaven is ever on the air, what tragedy that most of us should only, at best, catch fleeting strains of diviner music as we range up and down the dial listening for horse races and foxtrots.

What are you catching in the radio of your heart? What programs do you broadcast from the set of your soul? Do your children ever hear the finer things, the eternal features on the program of time, or do they catch nothing from you but the trivial advertisements of the temporal? Do your neighbors ever know that you tune in on heaven? When you visit and talk with men about you, what is the theme? How pitiful that we should pass through this world so full of opportunities to broadcast God and yet those around us never hear from us a voice of heaven.

Someone greater than the president is "on the air." The God of all the earth is broadcasting. Yield your little heart radio to Him and keep tuned in. When care and trouble and temptation would move the dial, keep ever on your guard that no other program ever shall come through. And, above all things, don't put up a station of your own and send our your own programs! Your business is to rebroadcast God.

I like to think that heaven will be a fair city where one, walking along the streets, shall never catch any strains of evil, but from every dwelling place shall ring out one happy chorus of praise to Him who has redeemed us. No discords of sin and heartache and trouble but everywhere the harmony of lives perfectly attuned to God!

What is going out over the air from your house and your heart? Are you broadcasting God?

September 30, 1931

11

Complete in Christ

Recently while reading advertisements in a psychology magazine, I was struck with the countless fads and schemes and systems now on the market, guaranteed to give inner harmony, victory over fear and worry, abounding happiness and success. This befuddled generation, so spiritually incoherent and dissociated, clutches at any sort of doctrine that promises soul unity and triumphant living.

Twenty centuries ago one lived among us the ideal life and gave us its secret. It is not necessary to go elsewhere now to find it for only He has it, and it is as available as ever.

The Bible verse "My God shall supply all your need according to his riches in glory by Christ Jesus" (Phil. 4:19) is not the extravagant claim of an enthusiast; it is plain, demonstrable fact.

In Jesus, as we accept Him, follow Him, share His Spirit and life, every need in human life—individual or collective—is supplied. As Paul put it, we are "complete in him."

Every need at which these modern fads are aimed, mental harmony, mastery of fear, worry, and vicious habits, forceful personality, health, and happiness—all these were met and answered long ago in Christ. They are all phases of the abundant life He came to reveal. It is easy for us to become obsessed with one particular phase of this life, fly off at a tangent, and making the part greater than the whole, run off into lopsided theories of mental healing, autosuggestion, and the like. But in Christ all these elements find their place in one glorious unity.

Whatever your need, it is met in Christ. If you are a mystical sort, He was Son of God and can lead you to the deepest secrets of the life in the Spirit. If you are a practical type, He was Son of Man who went about doing good, and His is a challenge to definite deeds of faith active in love. If you are of a sociable disposition, He was called a glutton and winebibber, and compared His gospel to new wine. If you are inclined to be serious, He was a man of sorrows and acquainted with grief.

The lighthearted find an easy yoke, and the troubled learn the true meaning of the cross. The harassed find peace; the sick, health; the sinful, forgiveness; the weak gain strength; the timid, courage; the simple, wisdom; the adventurous find the challenge of faith; philosophers find the ideal view of life; statesmen find the answer to every social need. He came, not to destroy, but to fulfill; and we are complete in Him.

Naturally, the aesthetic will talk of the beauty of the Christ life, the practical of the joy of service, and the philosophical will weave a Christian philosophy. Each of us will express what He means to us through the varied hues of our diverse temperaments. But let us exalt no private pet concept of Him above His many-sided fulness. For in Him all types find the ideal, and His Spirit radiates through all shades of human personality.

Why fool with any human theory—some partial, over-worked segment of truth? In Christ you have it all—in its true proportions—for "In him dwelleth all the fulness of the Godhead bodily."

And we are complete in Him.

January 18, 1931

35

PART 2

Determination

12

The Middle Mile

To most of us, the most important parts of a journey are the start and the finish. But the part of a trip that really tests the traveler is neither the beginning nor the end but the middle mile.

Anybody can be enthusiastic at the start. The long road invites you, you are fresh and ready to go. It is easy to sing then.

And it is easy to be exuberant at the finish. You may be footsore and weary but you have arrived, the goal is reached, the crown is won. It is not difficult to be happy then.

But on the dreary middle mile when the glory of the start has died away and you are too far from the goal to be inspired by it, on the tedious middle mile when life settles down to its regular routine and monotony—there is the stretch that tires out the traveler. If you can sing along the middle mile, you've learned one of life's most difficult lessons.

This is true of all life's little journeys. A boy hears a great musician and is inspired to undertake a musical career. Years later, he makes his debut and leaps into fame. Both those milestones, his start and his success, are played up in the papers. You hear nothing about the middle mile when he banged a piano until his ears rang, those dull, drab years when he was so often tempted to give it up and be a nobody. But it was the middle mile that made him, that proved the fabric of his soul. The middle mile is the testing mile in any art or trade.

A boy and girl marry. It is easy to be affectionate those first heavenly days when life is a paradise made for two. Fifty years later, they lie in the sunset's glow still in love although time has bent and wrinkled them and silver threads have long since replaced the gold. But it is neither the honeymoon nor the golden wedding that tests the lover. It is the middle stretch, when rent is due and hubby has lost his job and the kids have the whooping cough, that tests the traveler of the matrimonial highway.

A man is converted, "gets religion" we say. It is easy to be spiritual those first great days when the wine of a new affection so intoxicates the soul. A half-century later, he comes to the dark valley and a song is still on his lips and the heavenly vision is still bright within him. But the testing place of his religion was the long middle mile when the enthusiasm of the start had passed and the goal was still far away, when the vision had dimmed a bit and a "sense of things real came doubly strong." That is the test of your spirit!

So in life as a whole, it is not for fine beginnings and noble resolutions that we suffer most today. And nobody needs advice on how to be happy at the end of the road, for if you have traveled well, the end of the way will care for itself. It is on the intermediate stretch where the rosy start gives way to long desert marches, where the ordinariness of life bears heaviest on the soul—it is there that we need to know how to keep the inner shrine aglow with the heavenly vision. So many of us, in the words of the Master, begin to build and are not able to finish.

This grace of the middle mile the Bible calls "patient continuance." It is a wonderful art that few have mastered. It proves, as nothing else can, the character. And it gets least attention from the world because there is nothing very dramatic about it. There is something theatric in a big start or a glorious finish. There is nothing for a news reporter along the middle mile. It is a lonesome mile, for the crowd is whoopin' 'er up for the fellow who got through. It's a hard mile, for it's too far to go back and a long way to go on. But if you can keep a song within and a smile without on this dreariest stretch of life, if you can learn to transform it into a paradise of its own, you have mastered the greatest secret of victorious living, the problem of the middle mile.

January 16, 1927

13

The Positive Life

Some of us do not get anywhere in the building of character because part of us frustrates the rest of us. Our life is not a progress but a debate.

We set out to realize the ideal, and our best self votes in the affirmative. Straightway a number of contrary voices in our interior begin to protest, to argue, to filibuster against our decision. There is a critical point. Too often our best self, instead of going ahead with its program, stops to dally and debate with the conflicting elements; the conference of our inner selves becomes a noisy and confusing harangue, and we get nowhere.

Every man has in him positive and negative elements—high thoughts, clean ideals, noble purposes—everything that elevates the tone of life and strengthens its moral fiber is positive. But low and dirty thinking, perverse inclinations, unworthy desires, and everything that lowers the moral stamina, weakens the soul's morale, dulls the finer sensibilities, and makes the spiritual less real is negative.

What to do with this mixed-up Inside Congress is our problem. If we make a debating society of our inner lives we get nowhere, and our time is frittered away in internal strife. The only way out is to live positively. Decide upon the highest and worthiest course of action, gather all the positive elements behind it, and refuse to give the dissenters the floor.

Any man can tell which are the positives and negatives in his life. Let him give all his time to the positives, and the opposition will die from neglect. Let him cultivate wholesome and constructive thinking, helpful friends, good books, uplifting tastes and pursuits, and do only those things that build him up. The negatives will pop up all along—we cannot help—that but we can refuse to accept them, harbor, and encourage them.

Particularly in our thought life do we need to discriminate. Negative thoughts are the germs of the spiritual life that infect us with poisons that undermine our integrity and destroy our soul health. Just as in the physical world, some constitutions can throw off these microbes better than others, but none of us can afford to tolerate them, for the sturdiest will eventually give way if no action is taken.

All forms of fear, doubt, worry; all morbid, neurotic, unwholesome and vulgar tendencies; all moods, traits, and whims that endanger our spiritual vitality must be shunned. When they appear, meet and counteract them with a positive. That is "overcoming evil with good."

Do not dally with your inside congress. Vote your will for the best you know and start right in to carry the measure through. Hear only the affirmative voices and the negatives will die or line up with you. If you don't, the worst in you will veto the best.

The Bible preacher had this in mind when he said: "Whatsoever things are true, honest, just, pure, lovely, of good report, think on these things." Live positively!

May 12, 1929

14

Living by Proxy

One reason why so many of us live such drab and uninteresting lives is, we live by proxy. Most of our opinions, joys, and experiences are secondhand. Too stupid to play the game of life for ourselves, we sit in the grandstand and pay others to play it for us.

We go to the show and have our fun and romance vicariously. We don't try to find romance in real life; we think it exists only in novels or on the screen.

We go to the athletic field and pay others to play for us, while we sit hunched up with our indigestion and diabetes. Everybody ought to play part of the time and not some people all the time.

We go to school, and instead of learning there to think for ourselves, which is the only value of an education, we come away tanked up on other men's ideas, our heads crammed with odds and ends of information. And we go through life using other men's brains, mistaking information for education.

We go to the polls and vote, and most of us couldn't explain the difference between a Democrat and Republican for our lives. We usually vote like our granddaddies. Most of us are Democrats and Republicans for the same reason that we're Baptists and Methodists—it just runs in the family.

We go to church and listen to some man explain religion and pay him for it. But we never investigate religion for ourselves; never try it out in our own lives. As a result most of the religious opinions of men are secondhand conclusions borrowed from somebody else. Few people are personally acquainted with Jesus Christ. They have only heard of Him through an interpreter.

So we live by proxy—other people do our living for us. We do not go direct to the garden of life for our food, we live on mental and spiritual canned goods prepared in the laboratories of others. We live as a man might travel by changing from one train to another and never using his own legs. We never know the joy of original thought and independent living.

There is as much romance in your life as in any novel. Look for it. There is as much fun in your experience as Will Rogers or humorist George Ade find in theirs. Hunt for it. Life is a great game. You don't have to go to a stadium to see a fight. Your own life is a great scrap if you make it so. You have a head, use it for some other purpose than a hatrack. Don't limp through life on the crutches of other men's opinions. And don't depend on some preacher finding and explaining God for you. You are as near the Over Soul as any ecclesiastic. Truth and beauty and love and God are everywhere as the air and sunshine. Nobody has a monopoly on the eternal treasures, they are as free to you as to Coolidge or the pope of Rome or Henry Ford.

Quit living by proxy. Get out of the easy chair and walk on your own feet. Don't live a secondhand life!

December 26, 1926

15

Living in High Gear

The human machine is equipped with three gears. There is the low gear of the physical, of ordinary living. We eat and sleep and work and die, just like other animals. That is low gear, and most folks never get out of it.

Then there is the intermediate gear of the intellectual. We study, we become wise, we live by our heads instead of our hands, we learn to appreciate art and music and literature. That is intermediate gear, and many folks manage to get over into it but not anything like the many that stay in low gear.

And there is the high gear of the spirit. We move up from the intellectual into the spiritual; we find that only the eternal is real, and we live from the divine instead of the human point of view. That is high gear and few there are who reach it.

Most of us creep along like beasts of burden, living dull and drab and uneventful lives, untouched by beauty, bowed down by the dead weight of things. A few scramble up into a better state and manage by education of the mind and culture of fine senses to make life a little more bearable. But few indeed are they who shift into life's highest gear and move triumphantly through this world like princes.

There is no magic about it. Living in high gear is not the fortune of a favored few. Everybody has a high gear—the trouble is, they don't use it. It is all a matter of living in your higher self. The dumbest mortal has a better self. He may choke it and smother it, but it will keep reminding him at odd intervals that it is there. Perhaps he is afraid to try living in this other self—it seems so strange and new and different. Maybe he is afraid folks will think he is crazy, which they surely will. Or he may be so drunk with the coarse delights of his animal self that he wants nothing better. Anyway he goes groveling along like a galley slave when he might live like a king. Perhaps getting into intermediate gear would help to open his eyes. Certainly, if he would only dare to shift into high, he would be a new man.

Are you grinding along this rugged road of life in low, smoking and sputtering and knocking? Snap out of it! Grab the lever of your will and shift into high! It may scare you half to death; it may hurt a little; and the old beast may bounce and rear and shake you up mightily for a spell, but stay right in there. And you will begin to be conscious of new power—more power—mighty power—power that you never dreamed of before. And don't shift back into low either. The human machine doesn't call for changing gears after you get into high. Neither do you have to slide into low when you strike a stiff grade or a steep hill; the high gear of the soul takes them all. Just keep that lever set, pray a little, grit your teeth, stay put, and you'll come out on the top of the ridge with God's breezes blowing in your face. And when you reach the Valley of the Shadow, the same old gear will take you through.

It works anywhere. Do you have to meet a man tomorrow that you dread? Are you self-conscious, pestered with that infernal inferiority complex? Just shift into high and sail right in. You may make some bad drives at the start but you'll find that it works. Learn how to meet each difficult situation in your best self.

Jesus lived in high gear. And since He passed this way, how many poor souls, all stuck and bogged and smoked up along the hills of time with gears stripped and bearings melted and out of gas, have taken heart again, have stopped at the gospel garage, and have moved out to climb the high hills of a new experience!

Quit blaming the Creator for giving you a sorry machine! Just shift your gears, and we'll go through in high!

March 6, 1927

16

The Victorious Attitude

Most of us make the mistake of trying to change our circumstances instead of changing ourselves.

We imagine that when we are rich or famous or living in Florida, we shall be happy. The real issue is not our surroundings but ourselves.

Here is a man who is sick, jobless, moneyless, worried, and blue. Two roads are open to him. He can grovel along in the rut (as most of us do), bemoaning his fate, blaming luck, grumbling at Providence. In that condition he certainly will not better himself and usually it leads to failure, insanity, or suicide.

He can take another attitude. He can brace up, throw back his head, reaffirm his faith in God and life and start over. Instead of dwelling on the fact that he is sick, he can lay hold of the healing resources of the Infinite. He can say: "I am not jobless, I am helping God to build His world; I am not poor, the eternal resources are at my disposal; I shall not worry and be blue, but cast my burden on God."

Mind you, such an attitude may seem very unreal at first. Actual circumstances may make it look ridiculous. He may feel that he is kidding himself—that he is posing a piece of hypocritical make-believe.

But think a minute. Such an attitude will not make him worse, that's certain. If he keeps up that attitude he will soon change his circumstances, nine times out of ten. And if they are the sort that won't change, what is a little thing like a circumstance to a man with a faith like that!

Either way it works. Critics say there is no objective God or spiritual resources; that such an attitude is a mere subjective condition of the mind, a trick of the imagination, a kind of autosuggestion of self-hypnosis. Never mind analyzing the process. We know it produces the highest kind of results. It is, therefore, right. We who depend upon God are called cases of arrested development, who try to get rid of their inner complexes and inhibitions by laying them upon an external, imaginary God. But the vindication of such faith is in the authentic results it produces.

This attitude of faith is an adventure. It is daring to face adverse circumstances with a frame of mind that seems foolhardy and absurd in what we fondly call the face of "facts." But what are facts? If this attitude delivers us, is it not a higher fact? It is a choice between two sets of facts.

Most of us try to get through our dilemmas by mere stoicism or "doing the best we can." But unless we try faith we are not doing the best we can. Some worry and grieve along, some "wear it out," some grow sour and cynical, some give up and die. Against all these the glorious attitude of faith rings its challenge. But men, confusing faith with intellectual belief, see not hope.

Faith will triumph over any circumstances and conditions. For it shifts the center of life to the world of spirit, where circumstances mean nothing. The faith of a mustard seed will move mountains of adversity. And if it does not move the mountain, if sickness or poverty continue or death come, it will carry us over the mountain. The mountain will never overwhelm us.

As Shakespeare said in *Julius Caesar:* "The fault is not in our stars but in ourselves, that we are underlings." If dull reality looks insurmountable, meet it with another reality—faith. Remember, both are realities. One is seen, the other unseen. We act as if only visible circumstance were real. Spirit is the only reality. It is circumstance that shifts and vacillates. Don't get mixed up in your terms.

Don't be a slave to the lower realities. Meet them with the higher realities. And watch them fade.

June 9, 1929

17

Be Your Ideal

Do you have a mental picture of the person you would like to be: your ideal self? Do you cherish it, look at it once in a while, sigh and inwardly murmur, "Ah, why can't I be like that instead of the pale, one-cylinder nonentity that I am?"

Well, you can. But you won't be that ideal self so long as you merely carry it around as a mental picture to fondly contemplate now and then. It must be translated out of dreams into deeds, and that is not so easy.

If you would be your ideal, first form a definite and clear idea of what it is you wish to be—the sort of personality you want to become. A slipshod ideal means a haphazard and unsatisfactory realization.

Then, start right in the morning being that ideal self, instead of the old failure you have been up to now. It won't be easy and it will seem dreadfully unnatural at first and you will be tempted a thousand times a day to drop back into the old and easier rut. But whether you feel like it or not act like that ideal person you have wished to be. Even in the most trivial matters—for perhaps they matter most—hold the pose and handle every matter that comes along in attitude and activity according to the person you have chosen to be.

Of course you will make errors and your decisions will sometimes land you in dutch. The neighbors may think you have gone off-key a little and wonder what has happened. Let them wonder; that is part of the game. If you do lapse occasionally back into the old self and get caught off your base, and in unguarded moments act before you think, don't worry over it. Snap back into your new self and concentrate doubly strong.

If you do this, a wonderful thing will take place. Gradually you will become like your new self; the old will drop off little by little, until finally it becomes more natural to act like your new self than it did to run in the old rut. For whatever we practice long enough will become real.

There is nothing fictitious about this. We become artists,

musicians, athletes, orators, businessmen, experts in any line by acting like experts until we become masters. And characters are grown in the same way.

Good Christians are made in the same way. They are not suddenly transformed into Christlike characters. It is a gradual development as one makes Christ the ideal and daily lives as He would instead of in one's own way. That is what the Bible means by "looking unto Jesus," "putting on Jesus," and so forth. We make Him the ideal and live daily from His viewpoint instead of our own. And as we do that we gradually are changed into His likeness.

It is easy to cherish a fond mental photo of the self we want to be. It is not difficult to worship Jesus as a splendid ideal. But actually being like that ideal day by day in the office or among the pots and pans is the supreme test.

Be your ideal. There is no other way to its realization.

August 31, 1930

18

Second Wind

Psychologists speak of a "second wind" of inner resources. The phrase, of course, comes from the race course. A runner is almost exhausted; every nerve is taut, the last ounce of strength is fast dwindling. Suddenly the goal looms in sight! From the sidelines rises a storm of cheers! And from somewhere the racer lays hold of reserve power he did not know he had, and in a last mad dash sweeps through to triumph. He found his second wind!

Something like this was in the mind of Woodrow Wilson, during his strenuous years of public service, when someone suggested that he might wreck his constitution. "Constitution!" the president replied, "I'm living now on my by-laws!"

Psychologists tell us that when a man has reached the limit of his strength, has absolutely drained the reservoir of his stamina, he may fall back upon a reserve fund that normally never is tapped or else connect with unseen resources and carry through even stronger than before. He may catch his second wind.

But the deepest secret of this second strength is not hidden in physiology or psychology. A great Bible preacher said "When I am weak, then am I strong." This preacher had some sort of depressing weakness which he called his "thorn in the flesh." It harassed him, cut down his power, so he thought. But to his prayer for its removal, God answered "My strength is made perfect in weakness." That seems a strange doctrine in this age of fitness and efficiency, but it is the principle of the second wind. Only when a man come to the end of his own little inch does he reach the beginning of God's infinity. Man's extremity is God's opportunity and sometimes He lets us exhaust our little capital, wear out our pitiful endurance, that we may catch second wind from the resources of His Spirit. For when we are weak in ourselves we are strong in Him.

Most of us run poorly the race that is set before us because we run upon our first wind. There is a dependence, perhaps unconscious, upon our own faith, our own endurance, our own goodness. We are "all of self, none of Him." And one may run well that way after the fashion of this world. We may prosper materially, be held in good reputation, achieve a fair moral character. But it is not the Christ life. It will be well for us if our earthly props are all swept aside and we lose our first wind. Sometimes a man must be thrown upon his back before he will look up. Then we may see how helpless and undone we are, how insufficient our gasping strides, and lay hold upon the hidden reserves of the Eternal.

Paul ran well, as the world goes, upon his first wind. Brilliant, promising, gifted, and self-righteous—how he was forging ahead! Then one day his first wind played out. On the Damascus road he collapsed. But that day he caught his second wind that carried him through a stormy career of preaching and prison, stonings and shipwrecks, troubles and triumphs to eternal victory. His Resource never failed. "All these other things—my first wind—I count but loss," said he.

What a secret we have in the Lord! The weaker in ourselves, the stronger in Him. The more we suffer, the sweeter we sing. The greater our trouble, the brighter our triumph. The world cannot say that, for when its first wind is exhausted it has no other.

Said Professor William James; "There is a state of mind known to religious men, but to no others, in which the will to assert ourselves and hold our own has been displaced by a willingness to close our mouths and be as nothing in the floods and waterspouts of God. In this state of mind, what we most dreaded has become the habitation of our safety and the hour of our moral death has turned into our spiritual birthday. The time for tension in our soul is over, and that of happy relaxation, of calm deep breathing, of an eternal present with no discordant future to be anxious about, has arrived."

Second wind! Have you found it?

October 28, 1934

51

19

From Self to Service

Most of us are confirmed, self-centered egotists. We are continually petting and coddling ourselves. When we have a headache or the blues or lose some money or get insulted, we act as though we were the only persons to whom such a thing had ever occurred. We magnify our ills and misfortunes and forget that our woes are a tiny drop in the great ocean of a common human experience.

What happens to you and me doesn't matter much. Next time you have a flat tire or have to go to the hospital, don't imagine you are the only person who ever had such luck. Look all around you and you'll see thousands with flat tires and inhaling the ether, and most of them usually have flatter tires or worse appendixes than you. As a matter of fact such things as those—trouble, hardship, pain, disaster—are purely incidental matters and not worth half the importance we attach to them.

The important thing is not what happens to you, but what you cause to happen in life. The real object of our existence is not to see how long we can live, how well we can keep the old body machine knocking along, how many years we can stay here. Plenty of folks live more in thirty years than others in eighty. It is not how long but how *well* you lived that counts. How we fare personally is secondary; what matters is that we produce some worthy contribution to the world we live in.

The best way to get over self-centered living is to select some congenial and worthwhile work and spend the energy you would consume pampering yourself upon some labor of love for the betterment of the world in which you live. Set out to produce a good book or great music; to teach youth or befriend the friendless; to relieve pain or preach the gospel; to raise better vegetables or dignify politics; any work that adds to the sum total of human welfare and the glory of God is a work of art whether it concerns pigs, politics, or poetry.

Whatever your chosen expression, give yourself to it. Wear out yourself in it. Of course, take care of your body and mind but do not make that an end to itself. Care for yourself only that you may do better your greater work. The egotist gets no further than looking out for himself; he is his own ideal and life objective. But we are really functions rather than ends of creation. To stop with one's self is to live as a stagnant pond with no outlet; to truly live is to be a human stream flowing toward a greater sea.

The artist who froze to death with his coat wrapped around his statue may be fictitious, but he illustrates our truth. It is the law of self-sacrifice. Make your work the main thing and spend yourself that your masterpiece may live. That is the record of the great souls of all time—they sacrificed themselves for something greater. This principle finds its highest example in Jesus crucified for all mankind.

This way of living for something greater than yourself takes away much of the worry and strain of life. Petty bothers and concerns for one's self such as vex the self-servers do not fret these greater souls. They are careful to keep themselves in good trim if they may. But if adverse circumstance and condition overtake them they are resigned. They know that they themselves are incidental and are willing that the grain of wheat may die that the better harvest may come.

It is in this way that we pass from self to service, and losing our own self-lives find ourselves again glorified in the betterment of all mankind.

August 4, 1929

20
Practice Makes Perfect

All of us know that the way to be a good cook or baseball player or speaker is by practice. But we somehow can't get it into our heads that good Christians are made in pretty much the same way.

We agree that "practice makes perfect" in all realms except the religious. There we think things go by some other law. The life in the spirit is supposed to be a strange, vague, capricious affair of miracles and mysteries. And some of us waste much time and effort trying to share spiritual integrity as though it were some elusive will-o'-the-wisp to be caught with a fancy net.

But a Christian character of sturdy and enduring fiber is achieved along the same practical road of ceaseless practice. In a very real sense, good Christians are produced like good cooks—by hard work.

Of course, in either case, there must be the initial inspiration. But in the world of religion, as in any other, inspiration must be worked out in perspiration. A good Christian is not the fantastic creation of ethereal theories; he is the concrete result of plain laws of cause and effect.

No one ever became a great musician by merely reading about music, dreaming and praying about harmony, reveling in the lives of music masters. If ever he is to be a virtuoso, he must get down to tedious scales and exercises, monotonous drudgery, dull routine. It is strenuous and tiresome and not at all romantic; but it is the narrow way that leads to freedom.

So in religion we sing and pray and listen to fine sermons and read books that thrill the soul, which is well enough in its place, but we get no further. We look in the mirror and going away we straightway forget what manner of person we were, as James puts it. We wish we were good, we pray to be good, but we think it comes down from heaven or is achieved by some weird sort of spiritual calisthenics. We never substitute backbone for wishbone and work it out.

I quoted from James. He goes on to say: "But whoso looks

into the perfect law of liberty and continues therein, he being not a forgetful hearer but a doer of the word, this man shall be blessed in his doing." The ideal is worked out in daily practice; theory is translated into technique. It is often dull and tiresome and unromantic and discouraging. One does not always feel like shouting. Sometimes it appears that little is being done. But gradually and imperceptibly stronger faith, sturdier will, deeper loyalty, greater endurance grows out of the process, and we find one day resources we never dreamed were there.

If you want to be a real Christian, go to work. Live up to the best you know, act like your better self, meet each situation in Christ's spirit as best you can, no matter how awkward or unreal or how big a failure you make it. Naturally you will not fare like an expert. Don't expect to. If you played your first piece like a master, success would come too easily. But practice your faith everywhere: when you are alone, in public, with your friends, and at home with the family (where it is often hardest). And don't measure yourself every day to see how much you have grown. Just keep your eyes on the Master and your hands at work, and the miracle will happen—for it happens all along.

Did you say that takes the supernatural out of the Christian experience? Isn't there something supernatural about how a boy grows into a man? Isn't there a mystery in how practice makes a Paderewski? We have not removed the mystery, we have only put it where it belongs, in God's hands. How any man can become a good Christian is always partly a miracle; but the miracle is God's part of the process, not ours. And many of us never become good Christians because we try to do the miracle part instead of the work.

January 19, 1930

21

A Religion of Ruggedness

This ice-cream-soda generation is showing up its softness in religion as well as elsewhere. The sturdy hardihood of Puritan ancestors who braved a new continent, bitter winters, Indians, and starvation for God's sake, has passed; we recline in cushioned pews while a comfortable gospel toned down to match a bottle-fed world is served in delicious desserts from a silver platter.

The religion of Jesus calls us to no pleasant, hymn-singing excursion. There was nothing soft about Him. He grew up in a country village, sunburned and muscular from outdoor living, mingled with toil in a woodworker's shop. He led a rugged life, preaching in the open, sleeping where He had a chance. He fared hard clear through long strenuous days of teaching and healing, nights alone in the hills, tiresome foot journeys, and finally the ordeal of an awful death.

Nowhere in the Gospels do we catch the notes of modern cushioned living. Rather, Jesus calls us to take up a cross; to renounce self; to forsake parents and lands and goods; to cut off whatever imperils us, however dear; to lose our lives if we would find them; to count the cost of discipleship before we undertake it; to be servants, to brave persecution, to build on the rock, to endure to the end, to overcome the world. His challenge is always to a rough and rugged adventure that means hardship and struggle and strenuous living.

Whoever started the idea that Jesus was a softspoken idealist? He blazed out in wrath on Pharisees; was indignant at hard hearts; declared it better that a man be drowned with a millstone around his neck than that he offend "one of these little ones"; cleared out a gang of profiteering temple-traders; called a king a fox; and said to a close friend, "Get behind me, Satan"; condemned hypocrites who robbed widows and prayed long prayers; deplored a religiousness that called Him *Lord* and did not His commands; and frankly rebuked a sentimentalism that said fine things but did not "hear the word of God and keep it."

A real Christian is no grinning Pollyanna, all smiles and sentiment. He is a rugged, sturdy soul who is under no illusions about life and is grappling with things as they are. He is not always agreeable and sweet, for he must be uncompromising and firm amidst a superficial world. He is no lamblike creature forever mumbling prayers and universally pleasant. He is a battle-scarred warrior who does not confuse singing the anthem with fighting the good fight.

We have thought mistakenly of a Christian as a soft, sheepish, tender goody. But the real heroes of faith are weather-beaten, husky, battered fellows who have shown us that one can be a dare-saint as well as a dare-devil. Real Christians spend little time dreaming and wishing and have no use for those who would imagine the kingdom in; they are up and about wrestling with unlovely reality. It is not always nice and pleasant work and they do it imperfectly and are not at all ideal folks, but they are the people Jesus valued most for, though rough, they are genuine.

Being a Christian means being game for God's sake, husky for heaven's sake, rugged for righteousness' sake. Better be out in the scrimmage and make a thousand errors than sit on the sidelines in blissful piety and never risk your idealism in the clash with reality.

February 1, 1931

PART 3

Coping with Everyday Pressures

22

Stop, Look, and Listen

I don't suppose I'll ever be a front-page modern success. I am not the up-to-date, gate-crashing, efficient, go-getter type. I am not the hustling, up-and-about, businesslike live wire headed for a limousine and the boss's daughter.

I grew up in these hills where living has not become a fever. I have not been in such a hurry that I cannot stop along the road to pick a violet, to listen to the wood thrush, or watch the silent mystery of sundown. The race is not so tense that we must miss all the beauty of the journey with our eyes fixed upon a goal.

What is the idea in the frantic rush? There is nothing at the end of that track but high blood pressure and insomnia. Why hurry to get to that?

So the more progressive sort deplore my lack of "pep." I am not aggressive; I do not take the initiative; I am a clod. I ought to get out and put over something. I am dumb, talking about sunsets and birdsongs in this great age of stocks and bonds and dividends!

Somehow when I watch the kind that live among such things and listen to their chatter I don't feel that I've missed much. How those, fretted, frenzied mannikins need a good dose of woodland air, the breath of pines, the lure of a lake in the full moon, the serenity of a cabin by a creek, the tonic of tramps in snow, the melody of a hermit thrush, the thrill of a summer sunset!

Railroad crossings used to warn us to STOP, LOOK, AND LISTEN. Many physical, mental, and spiritual wrecks might be averted if we obeyed that injunction along all the trail of life.

Stop! You are straining yourself to death chasing dirt and dollars. Check up, mop your brow, sit down, and rest awhile. Take stock of yourself; your life is all disarranged; the wrong thing is at the top of the list. Your sense of value is out of focus. Get your breath and think. You are running because everybody else is. There is no sense to it—they just got started and everybody is afraid to quit for fear of being rated a back number. And yet every one of them wants to take it easier, but they've got into the swing and can't break out. Put first things first, rearrange your interests according to their true importance, and laugh at yourself for being such a nut.

Look! The drama of life is unfolding around you every day, more wonderful by far than all our superficial little creations. Watch the pageant of the seasons, the witchery of bud and brook and blossom, and people themselves—as they are, not polished up in plays and pictures. What is so fascinating as the comedy and tragedy of day by day?

Listen! The whisper of the zephyr, the tumult of the west wind; the winged choir of the woods; the music of men from the ditty of a child to the nocturnes of Chopin; the voice of God through the sounds of earth, hear Him above the squawking of this racketty age.

Stop, Look, Listen! Whether you make your pile or not, get into society or on the front page or into *Who's Who* is purely incidental. What matters is whether amid the scramble you knew how to stop; whether amid the shortsightedness and blindness you know how to look; whether amid the clatter and the chaos you listen for the voice of God.

March 30, 1930

23

Lopsided

We are informed that Will Rogers got $12,500 for a speech. Babe Ruth draws $80,000 a year. Amos 'n' Andy make $75,000 or $100,000. We also have several million who make nothing and do well to draw their breath. I believe we call them "unemployed."

We do not here revile the supersalaried set. Will Rogers is the Court Jester of America, and his reflections upon this modern comedy called congress are, alone, worth good pay. But, of course, no speech ever was worth $12,500. That is simply one of the jests of progress.

For baseball we hold no brief. It is merely one of the insanities with which a dyspeptic and bottle-fed generation vainly tries to stave off the boredom and ennui of a vapid life.

"Amos 'n' Andy" must be credited so far with a clean show, which is more than most modern entertainments can boast.

But we are driving at a principle, not personalities. It is a lopsided state of affairs when one man can make that much money while millions look for work.

We have heard much of the scarcity of money. There is as much as ever. Nobody has burned it up. It simply has become centralized in the hands of a few who have enough to spend a fortune on one show, while multitudes wear out their lives counting nickels to make ends meet. That "the rich grow richer and the poor poorer" is a truism. We may well expect discontent and unrest when thousands who love their kiddies as well as the prosperous love theirs read and hear of such financial avalanches in some quarters while the wolf is already halfway in their door.

Nor is it a matter of merit. Another generation will never know that most of our supersalaried ever lived, while the greatest geniuses of this day may just now be faring on crackers and cheese. A sexy musical comedy can pull down enough to start a bank, while hundreds of ministers of the gospel—clean, fine souls, the sort that keeps this world together, the moral cement and salt of the earth—live on salaries that are a disgrace to the well-fed brethren who adorn the amen corner.

We know that money is not everything but it is something. There is no better index to the spirit and mind of this age than the way it spends its money, who gets it, and what they get it for. Can we be surprised that our youth get from example the idea that the old plodder is out of it, while the new success is the fellow who can put over the cleverest trick?

Of course those of us who have set out to live for things that really matter are not deceived. Our treasure is elsewhere and we are not seriously upset by the price our stuff brings in modern markets. But it is confusing to unsettled and immature minds, these unfair and absurd present standards of value.

It's a strange U.S.A. And to cap the joke we carry "In God We Trust" on our coinage. But we trust in money, in luck, in looks, in wit and shrewdness—in everything but God. What's the use lying about it?

April 6, 1930

24
Watch Your Step

Sometimes strolling out the old road here at home I look across the hills and think for a long time about this odd little trip we call *living*. Usually I come back feeling that the wonder of it is not that some break down but that so many of us get through as well as we do.

How uncertain is our breath! Is it not almost a miracle that we can move through disease, germs, dodge automobiles, survive tornado and flood, and get by a thousand lurking unseen dangers to reach sixty, eighty, even one hundred years? This frail little framework of flesh and blood amid our modern perilous complexities looks like a baby in a jungle but on the average it does incredibly well.

What about this strange little device called *brain* and *mind*? A delicate instrument, easily broken, yet most of them keep in good enough shape to get us by the bughouse.

Doubly true is this when our moral integrity is considered. If ever keeping clean and good was a tight-rope walk, it is today. Moral morasses and swamps of spiritual peril stretch before us so insidious and complicated that it is a marvel so many spirits carry through to a glorious finish.

> Alas, how easily things go wrong!
> A sigh too deep, or a kiss too long,
> And then comes a mist and a weeping rain,
> And life is never the same again.
> George MacDonald

How terribly true! No life is safe until the very last step has been taken. In youth we must master fiery passions and break wild impulses to the bit of discipline. And how many fail there the newspaper records of crime and suicide but faintly indicate. But maturity does not mean safety; it merely changes the nature of the perils. Success knows perhaps more dangers than obscurity, and the old are doubly imperiled by the very self-confidence of him who "thinketh he standeth" when he is about to fall.

There is no safe ground. We must watch our step. When our footing is so precarious there is but one thing to do: commit ourselves to the best we know and carefully live up to the light we have. That calls for circumspect living. Nowadays we laugh at the word *circumspect*. It has a poor reputation. The world glorifies the reckless and extravagant. "Eat, drink, and be merry" is the slogan and the modern collapse in character shows just where such a fool philosophy leads. To be sure, one can be circumspect to a fault, but we are in no danger of becoming extremists there.

To live meticulously, measuring every step before taking it, would reduce life to a mechanical routine without tone and color. We do not mean that. Long ago One came who threaded His way through this labyrinth to a fine finish. He fell into no snares; He kept the high road; He lived ideally in this tedious world. And His life was no dreary monotone but suffused with music and light.

Let us live as He did; make Him the Ideal; face life in His Spirit, live it His way. The creeds are no pale and insipid legalism once we are infected with His Spirit. Life without Him nowadays is a dangerous and hopeless procedure. Life with Him retains all its charm and romance; it does not grow drab as the critics sneer. It grows lighter for His yoke is easy and His burden light. And the Way grows clear as we travel, for if in all our ways we acknowledge Him, He will direct our paths.

February 2, 1930

25

Moneyized Music

I am one of the millions of radio bugs who labor evening after evening trying to drag in from the world of other some tune or talk as a sort of romantic and glamorous ending for another day.

I get plenty of music—worlds of jazz, some classical selections, now and then a hymn. It is a wondrous thing, the magic of the old masters drifting in to me from the Great Unseen. I like to turn out the light and leave only the firelight so that the radio is invisible. That adds to the enchantment.

But one feature of the program gets my goat. I hate to hear some divine masterpiece end up with this announcement: "This program is sponsored by Thunderbolt and Company, makers of high-grade left-hand monkey wrenches. Their slogan is 'Wrenches for every nut.'"

Imagine Beethoven over in the spirit world hearing his sonatas employed to advertise soap! Bach has become a press agent for peanut butter, and Chopin is used to recommend carpet tacks! Wagner sells chewing gum, and Schubert makes ads for sewing machines!

It is another mark of a commercialized age. Nothing escapes the taint of it. Even the sacred world of song is not immune. The immortal dreams of by-gone masters who almost starved to death for their artistic devotion are sacrificed on the altars of Mammon. A money-mad age without soul and conscience puts Schumann and Liszt upon broadcasting soapboxes to lure with their immortal melodies the populace to the slot machines.

One does not mind hearing jazz so employed. Even that use is an honor to jazz. But the classics—ah, that is another matter.

Some see it all in a different light. It is a good sign, they say. Modern business has joined hands with great music. The wall of partition has fallen; money and melody walk together. Instead of music being moneyized, money is being musicalized. Art and business are wed, the dreamer and doer now work together.

But I "hae me doots." Josef Hofmann deplored the tendency toward lowering music to the crowd instead of lifting the crowd up to great music. This modern policy smacks of degradation, not exaltation. Music is not glorified but commercial products are. The immortals are debased to an unworthy use.

Must it be done to finance the programs? I believe I'd rather we'd pay tax enough to cover the classics or let advertising be done by jazz. Nothing much would be lost for almost everybody is hunting for jazz anyway. But give us poor back numbers our Wagner without the washing machines and our Beethoven without blanket ads.

Of course, it's all in the way you look at it. It does seem discordant to be lifted out of yourself by the witchery of "Minuet in G" only to fall with a thud when into the vision the artist has created comes crashing some announcer telling you the virtues of Fitzpatrick Alamagoozlum's new remedy for frostbite.

I may be alone in my taste and will be promptly labeled one of the old-timers who hasn't caught up. I don't suppose most of the radio bugs care what happens to Brahms and Mendelssohn so long as there's a fox-trot with every turn of the dial.

November 25, 1928

26

A Rustic Protest

I live beside a dirt road. I have heard recently that it may sometime soon become a modern, up-to-date, hard-surface highway, thereby bringing to my door all the advantages and glories of present-day travel.

Which news fails to send me into hallelujahs or to evoke from my chest one hooray. I ain't enthusiastic. I don't know as how I hanker after a highway by my door.

There may be advantages therein. I could see many fancy autos and have the honor of residing along a busline and glimpse license plates from far and away as citizens from remote states sped by.

I took to the country that I might partly escape the hydra-headed monster of modernity but I fear I must reassemble my effects and dig deeper into the woods lest the ogre still consume me.

I'm about as modern as I care to be. I hear enough knocking engines and smell enough defunct gas and witness enough hurrying to and fro to suit me. If my road is improved and five times the present quota is poured along the thoroughfare, I shall be tempted to erect detour signs above my location and below.

The woods have been cleared around my domicile and traffic has increased until I have to walk a mile to see a wood thrush or a warbler. And I had rather reside within easy distance of a couple of cardinals than see a Pierce-Arrow every thirty minutes.

Our greatest disadvantages nowadays are our advantages. Everything we do to simplify life complicates it. We thought automobiles would simplify transportation, and they have befuddled it. The same is true with every other field. We have invented machines to make life easier and better regulated, and now we are up to our ears in engines and cog wheels and in a worse puzzle than ever. We have built up a vast system and neglected ourselves and now we have nobody with brains enough to understand and operate the system.

I think there is a chance for me if I can avoid most of our improvements. I may be able to retain what little sense I have if I can steer clear of this advanced knowledge. I had the good fortune to not get a college education. There is one advantage in going to college—most folks go when they are young so they have the rest of their lives in which to get over it.

I hate to see anything approaching that threatens to desecrate the sanctity of these hills. I have striven all my life to avoid being a modern, up-to-date citizen. But the improvers have conspired against me.

So if you stop at my place and find me on a modern highway with the buses whizzing by, do not congratulate me—rather console me. You will find me in disgrace, my pride and self-respect gone, reduced to the pitiful plight of a progressive, up-to-the-minute citizen.

February 3, 1929

27
How Shall We Live?

A Hawaiian chief was given some pills to take, one each hour. The first one helped him so much, he took all the rest at once and almost died.

Nobody will ever know just how much time and energy has been wasted, and how much misery has been caused by the fool habit of trying to understand life and gulp it down at the start before we live it. We wear out our brains inventing innumerable ways to live, instead of letting life unravel as we go along. Life must be taken in regular doses if we are to be healthy and wholesome.

After thousands of years of speculation and philosophizing, the happiest people are not the bewildered geniuses who rack their brains over the riddle of existence. The elect of earth today are the simple and unspoiled common folks who accept life and keep so busy living it that they have no time for morbid and neurotic vagaries.

I have spent a good many years with my nose buried in books, trying to analyze the universe just as every thinking youngster will do in his teens and twenties. I've almost scratched all the hair off the top of my head studying the roadmaps of life when I should have been enjoying more of the journey. And at twenty-five I have learned that of the making of books there is no end, and much study is a weariness of the flesh. I have listened to preachers and philosophers galore and read enough on how to live to stock a library. And I've reached this conclusion:

There are only a few things that a man needs to know to start with, and the rest he will learn as he goes. A simple faith in God; appreciation of nature; respect for yourself and consideration for others; a job you like to work at; a good wife and a couple of babies; a liver that isn't torpid; and a sense of humor—these constitute the fundamentals of sane and wholesome living. Give a man these, and while he may not be up on modern philosophy and a poor authority on Schopenhauer, he will rate a thousand times higher than the sophisticated perverts who laugh at life's simplicities and starve on intellectual sawdust.

The present wave of suicide and insanity and crime has many of its roots in the fact that modern youth, in its feverish search for elaborate philosophies of life, has trampled underfoot the simple things which alone can give us that for which we agonize and pray. We are laughing today at elemental truths of home and love and God in our conceit. But for all our wit and erudition we are a miserable crowd, and the sooner we give up chasing neurotic fancies and return to the great simplicities, the better.

After all, the ideal person in this country is not the tousleheaded visionary who spends his days contemplating the puzzle of life and never knowing what it means to live. The greatest character is the ordinary chap who was lucky enough to be reared poor and by hard work, who has his ideals grounded in good common sense, who works for a living, has a home and a family, and takes each day as it comes. The intelligentsia may deplore his stupidity, and the sophisticates may sneer at him because he has never been enough of a genius to contemplate suicide, but his is the only philosophy of life that has ever given real satisfaction.

Some of our self-styled idealists and dreamers, who think they have solved the problem of existence, are really suffering from indigestion brought on by a sedentary life. Some of the poor devils who are tearing their hair over the dilemmas of their own imagination really need a year's vacation in the mountains or a sensible wife who can turn them from writing poetry to writing checks. If some of our modern reformers who are trying to run the universe could be put to rocking a cradle, they might recover from their obsession, and we common folks would be able to muddle along in peace.

July 17, 1927

28

I Philosophize

Part of the human race is engaged in having a good time, and the other part is cussing them out for having so much fun. If the joy chasers would use a little more sense and the joy killers a little more sentiment, what a world this would be! One bunch is too arid, and the other is too acrid. But that's human nature—when you set out to have a good time, you lose your head, and when you undertake to live sensibly, you lose your heart.

It is true that variety is the spice of life, but half of humanity is trying to live on spice and the other half without spice, and you can't do either. Some of us are trying to live on dessert, and we have become dyspeptic. You can't grow an athlete on cake and ice cream, and you can't build a character on knick-knacks.

I don't blame the modern girls for trying to be pretty by trying. It's a by-product.

I like the modern girl. Of course since I live a simple life I stand a poor chance of marrying any of them, for they are about as wild for complexity as for complexion. The new models are made for fast traveling. The modern girl is not interested in living by the side of the road—she's more interested in whizzing down the middle of the road.

Marrying is a dangerous business nowadays. You can't tell how it will pan out—some go crazy because they didn't get a wife, some because they did. I don't know why they play the "Wedding March" at church when folks marry. From the way many marriages turn out nowadays, the choir ought to sing "The Fight Is On."

I believe the Almighty put us here to enjoy life, not to explain it. Even the Good Master said that a child was His idea of a real character, and children don't analyze, they enjoy. Personally, I quit trying to run the universe several years ago, and started out to appreciate it. I've discovered that this is the most interesting world I've ever lived in. Stevenson was right:

"This world is so full of a number of things, I'm sure we should all be happy as kings."

Get out of the glooms, you muttonheads, Christmas is coming! We are suffering today because we are philosophizing away from life the spirit of mystery and romance, and life without that is like Christmas without Santa Claus.

Surely in a world so good as this, it is no crime to be happy!

December 19, 1926

29

The Athletic Mania

It is a sad day for education when the college hero is the football star instead of the valedictorian.

If the present athletic mania keeps up, my definition of a university as a football stadium with a college annex will be quite correct.

William Allen White is certainly justified in saying that the football tail is wagging the college dog, and Roger Babson has a right to deplore "big business athletics."

Bricks and brawn are becoming more important than brains. When a football coach can draw a bigger salary than a professor, when the center of interest is the gridiron instead of the classroom, can you wonder that a lopsided young generation is marching out of our colleges into life with a distorted and unbalanced standard of values? Can you wonder that the scale of life's interests is so miserably twisted and upset today, when the heaven of the average student is the athletic field and the star athlete is his god? When it is more desirable to be a fullback than it is to know the spiritual treasures of literature and history, can you expect anything but a return of the philosophy of the beast? When the physical is so exalted above the spiritual that a pigskin artist can draw more spectators than twenty preachers can draw listeners, the fault is not entirely with the preachers. When a young man can draw a larger salary and crash into the limelight far more quickly by having a big body than by having a big brain, don't be surprised if he gives up greatness for gridirons. One sympathizes with the father who said that he spent five thousand dollars on his boy's education and got only a quarterback.

When you consider the mob that turns out to any sort of physical combat and listen to the Comanche yell of several thousand fight fans, you can't help reminding yourself that, for all our radios and airplanes, we are still only a bunch of savages with a thin veneer of civilization. And if the present rage for the physical is not controlled and restricted to its proper channels, we are going to lose even the veneer.

I am no pessimist but whenever I see a modern stadium crowded with frenzied fight fanatics, my thoughts drift back to the amphitheaters of Rome in the days of her waning glory. And I wonder whether the experience of bloody centuries has taught us anything after all. Below the few surface and superficial changes there is little difference between modern America and decadent Rome.

No nation can last long when it stops praying and takes up playing. Of course, we ought to mix them but we don't. There has never yet been a nation that was able to retain in its days of prosperity the discipline and hardihood of its early adversities. America shows no signs of being an exception.

At first thought it might seem that the discipline of athletics would offset the growing softness of America. It does the opposite, for it takes only a tiny percentage of our manhood and makes athletic specialists of them in order to entertain the sluggish multitudes who are too lazy to play and prefer to pay others to play for them. When athletics is commercialized to amuse a stupefied generation of mushy dyspeptics, don't expect it to harden them. America is in the grandstand, getting softer all the time.

And anyway, the modern system of physical culture with its overstrain, its high pressure, its sudden tax on heart and nerves, is contrary to all principles of correct exercise. Instead of living in the open, exercising naturally, and building up a coordinated physique by regular methods, we work out in spasms in stuffy gymnasiums and build up a hulk of muscles (to be sure) but not a real physical specimen. The Indian had the modern athlete beaten all hollow.

Modern athletics has succumbed to the same commercializing spirit that threatens every phase of our civilization. And God save us when America is dominated by real estaters and fight promoters!

January 30, 1927

30

The High Cost of Pride

Our real problem is not the high cost of living but the high cost of keeping up with the neighbors. It is the upkeep of our inflamed egotism that is so expensive.

We buy cars we cannot afford, build homes beyond our means, and try to eat spring chicken on a hot-dog salary simply because the neighbor next door has done it, and we'll stay with them or bust. If someone on the same street comes out in a month's-salary frock, we sacrifice a two-months' income to get one jump ahead. So we gather around us a carload of junk we do not need, cannot pay for, and are better off without just because "they're all doing it," and, slaves of the herd, we must do it too.

We never stop to ask why we do it. If we had time in this insane race to halt, mop our brow, and look around, we might come to our senses and stop it. It is all a fool struggle without meaning or goal, a tussle of dumbbells who would rather lose their immortal souls than have Mrs. Jenks, the social matron, frown upon them. It is a sort of itch, easy to catch and hard to cure, that breaks out in card parties, pale teas, shin twistings, and other eruptions, and ends in the cancer of exclusiveness. Why anybody ever wants to get into such a nerve-racking, high-tension race is inexplicable but the fever of it runs through all the social strata from the dingalings of some back alley to the inmates of the most fashionable clubs.

Any man who will come out from this mob with sense and courage enough to live simply and let the Joneses rave will find that even today life is not such an ordeal. Life as God meant for us to live it is a desirable thing; it is we who have twisted it by our fool inanities into a senseless rush for tinsel trophies. God intended that we have more sense than to load ourselves with so much luggage that we cannot enjoy the journey simply because some other fool has set the example.

It is the cut-throat cost of luxuries, absurdities, and non-essentials that has our nose to the grindstone. Any man who will keep his nose there for lack of grit to live his own life ought to have the old proboscis ground off. We are a race of cowards dancing to a tune that is spelling bankruptcy, insanity, divorce, suicide, and a world of lesser ailments; we dare not quit for fear the neighbors label us wallflowers.

It is not the actual cost of living but the extravagant price of this crazy way of living that is driving us crazy. And yet we talk about "living your own life!" If ever there was a race of mortals more unanimously alike, more colorless and monotonous and all of one kind, it is the present crop. There is about as much individuality in the average run of fashion magazine perusers as in a chew of tobacco. And somebody had the nerve to start all this talk about "being different!" Who is different?

Church folks worship the same god. And pay to the church what is left over after the Saturday sacrifice uptown, while the dusty Bible on the shelf says, "Be not conformed to this world: but be ye transformed by the renewing of your mind."

September 21, 1930

31

The Delusion of Leisure

One of the stock arguments for this machine age is the threadbare contention that the machine will eventually set man free from grinding toil and slavish labor so that he can have abundant leisure in which to enjoy the finer things of life. We are to be emancipated from work into a fairyland of golf and grand opera.

Like most of the world's promises, the whole thing is a delusion. In the first place, the machine has not simplified life nor has it liberated man. The automobile was to simplify transportation; it has complicated it. The printing press would simplify writing; how it has plunged us into a wilderness of books with the hopeless question of which to read! The more devices we invent, the more baffling life becomes amongst them all!

Far from freeing us, the machine has bound us. The engine has shackled the engineer. We wear ourselves out moving from one labor-saving device to another! Men never were so mechanical, so stereotyped, so devoid of color and individuality, so uniformly standardized to a lifeless pattern, as today. We are dummies, automatons, soulless manikins of the modern Punch and Judy show. The machine has fettered, not freed, us.

In the second place, even if the machine did translate us from labor to leisure, what would we do with leisure if we had it? Only the busy are happy anyway. The most miserable mortals among us now are those with time to kill and money to burn. They tour hither and yon, from beach to mountain resort, in a whirl of dances and nightclubs, yachts and horse races, gamblings and divorces, and none look more pitifully tragic than these bored cynics, afflicted with leisure. As far as idleness enabling us to enjoy the finer interests is concerned, experience points up the other road. We shall have to produce a better grade of folks than ever has come along so far before we can even endure leisure, to say nothing of enjoying it. What would we do with it if we had it?

Nor does freedom from work enable the gifted to produce their masterpieces. The greatest creative works of the race have been wrung from toil and hardship. Whether one thinks of the founding of our nation in privation and suffering, or Beethoven's music born of fearful limitations, or Rembrandt's art baptized in adversity, he knows that our finest productions did not come from loungers in white flannels at some pleasure retreat. And when one turns to the higher works of God through men in the realm of religion, he knows that the Christian church was not born and grown in vacation shades. Indeed, when the Eternal took flesh and dwelt among us, He was no armchair dreamer, spinning airy abstractions. Instead, He declared "My Father worketh hitherto, and I work."

The ideal life is not a maximum of rest mixed even with a tiny minimum of business. We enjoy leisure only as we know the contrast of work. All work and no play may make Jack a dull boy but all play and no work has produced no satellites.

Loafing is no worthy ideal on earth or in heaven. The Master promised to give rest but with the next breath said "Take my yoke upon you and learn of me." We need yokes when we work. And when He pictured the rewards of the life to come He favored the faithful by making them rulers over many things, which implies responsibility and occupation.

The machine cannot free us, for freedom comes only through the Spirit. And spiritual freedom comes only through loyal obedience to Christ, the Liberator. "If ye continue in my word, then are ye my disciples indeed; And ye shall know the truth, and the truth shall make you free."

May 27, 1934

32
Putting the Christ In

The usual signs of approaching Christmas are with us again. Streets jammed with frantic buyers; shopkeepers feverishly raking in a landslide of dollars; bootleggers working overtime on holiday hootch; a hundred or so Santa Clauses speaking from every broadcasting station while children wonder which is the real thing.

A few more days and we shall be in the midst of it. We shall be getting gloves that don't fit and books we don't read; husbands will open cigars nobody on earth can smoke, and wives will receive exactly the kind of pearls they didn't want; Uncle Henry will get bedroom slippers, when he never wore a pair in his life, and somebody will be sending me a cigar lighter!

Modern Christmas has about everything but Christ. We have commercialized Jesus out of His own birthday.

We have an orgy of buying and selling. We have a fever of giving presents. That would be well enough but so many of us give *things* instead of giving ourselves. Some husband reading this will have spent a month's salary on a gift for the wife, when what she wants most is himself, his heart. She is dying for devotion, not diamonds. And some wife will buy hubby a trunkful of junk for Christmas and nag him into nervous prostration the rest of the year. Most of our giving is because we look for something in return—because it's customary. We send Mrs. van Snoodle something because we know she will remember us. We get Aunt Hephzibah some stationery, not because we love her, but because she is on the list and hasn't died yet.

How many of us will think of the Christ in Christmas? Oh, we shall go see the pageant at church or perhaps even take a perfunctory part, but were He to view it from the backseat, seeing our hearts as well as hearing our parts, would He be glorified?

Of course, we donate to a Christmas dinner for the poor— and let them shift the rest of the year as best they can. We grow generous and tip the beggar on the corner, send the sick man a book, help cheer the crowd in the jail. But we do not follow it up, and it is the follow-up that counts.

A lot of modern "Christmas spirit" is pure hokum. It is simply a temporary outburst of shallow sentimentality with which we excuse our failure to really follow the Christ. We will not actually make Him our Lord and live His spirit every day—it is so much easier to celebrate once a year with a spectacular demonstration that hides the very Christ it claims to honor. If we once set out to daily do His will, every day might be Christmas and every wayside bush a Christmas tree.

To say anything contrary to this annual ballyhoo is to be at once labeled a Scrooge, but we want a *genuine* Christmas spirit and not a pagan, sentimental craze that has been commercialized out of all reverence and spirituality.

Amid this wild orgy of traffic and trade, drink and dance, extravagance and excess, we have lost the Christ. We have exchanged Him for Santa Claus, substituted holly trees for His cross, the giving of things for the giving of self. Nothing else do we need so much this day as to put the Christ back into Christmas.

December 22, 1929

PART

Nature's Splendid Gifts

33
Back to the Woods

Modern commercialized athletics has practically killed the study and enjoyment of nature among our youth. A football contest will easily pack a stadium with howling fight fanatics, but a tramp in the woods in quest of birds or flowers is laughed at as a pursuit worthy only of children and old maids.

Camping and woodcraft have lost their charms for a bottle-fed generation that cannot do without its bedroom slippers and steam heat. And a crop of youngsters brought up on the artificial thrills of gymnasium exercise finds scant enticement in a proposed jaunt across the hills.

I have taken with me now and then on my outdoor perambulations various individuals, and I have frequently been disappointed and saddened at the utter blindness of so many to the real glory of the woods and hills and their deafness to the voice of nature. Often I have been reminded of the Bible verse: "But the natural man receiveth not the things of the Spirit of God: for they are foolishness unto him: neither can he know them, because they are spiritually discerned." Paul was not talking of outdoor life but the application fits. The Spirit of God speaks among the trees, and few there be who hear Him.

The woods were God's first temples, and we are much the poorer for not worshiping there more today. Many treasures await us that we never shall find indoors: health, exercise, beauty, clearness of mind and keenness of eye, spiritual strength and truth, lie in the fairyland of bud, bird, and brook. Most of our wretchedness and disease can be cured by a treatment of sunshine, air, water, and outdoor life mixed with spiritual understanding.

But we have grown so lazy that we pay professionals to exercise for us while we look on from the grandstand. And if we go in for modern athletic life, we shall probably be harmed more than helped. The physical value of it is questionable, while the other sides of it are conspicuous for their absence.

We belong to the outdoors. The Bible starts us out in a garden, and we have been wandering from that garden ever since.

Ceilings and bricks are the death of us. Rightly does the Seer of Patmos visualize the eternal home with trees and rivers. We do not want to get to heaven and find only skyscrapers.

Homes do not encourage nature study. I remember how my father opposed my studying birds until he saw the value in it. Schools give it trifling importance outside of a bug-hunting trip for biology or a grasshopper quest. Churches have forgotten that Jesus was an outdoors teacher and need tremendously to get out of their stone temples into the open air, so some of the hot air can blow out of modern Christianity. And an economic system that makes an outdoor trip only possible in a rare vacation strikes the finishing blow.

Let us get back to the woods if we can. Better be poor and know where the hermit thrush sings and the trailing arbutus grows than own a couple of skyscrapers and be nothing but rich, prosperous, and a success.

April 20, 1930

34

A Morning Ramble

I was out early this morning. I hope I may never belong to that class so afflicted with money as to be able to lie in bed after sunrise. Some call it a luxury. It is a crime. Such people gain nothing—and what they miss!

This morning I pulled on my woods garb, grabbed my stick, and was away down to a little meadow that lies along a baby creek. Every sprig and bush was mantled in frost, the whole meadow bejeweled as if in honor of the new day.

I stood a while in the crisp morning and lost myself in the world around me. That is an art well worth learning—how to glide out of the shell that people think is you, the paraphernalia of this modern life, how to lay aside the clownish trappings of business, and merge into that elemental world of sky, sun and sod, bird, brook and blossom, where you belong. It is a delightful thing to know how to lose your artificial identity and become an integral part of the woods.

I stood in the doorway of an old deserted cabin and watched the miracle of dawning. Soon, away in the east, the ruddy-faced sun, drunk on morning wine, hung his chin over the horizon to smile at a sleepy-eyed world. Far above me two trifling crows flapped lazily past a silver moon.

Oh, I do not care what else you may have done—you have not really lived until you have seen such sights as these!

Titmice, chickadees, and kinglets chatter through the trees. They seem to like each other's company—and cold weather. There is something brave, hilarious and challenging about the call of a titmouse that fascinates me. The chickadee is an incurable optimist. And how the tiny, fragile kinglet endures such weather is a wonder to me. But when it's too rough for everybody else it's just getting right for him.

Snowbirds are plentiful. Why do the bird books label him a "junco"? Such a name means nothing, but what the word *snowbird* expresses!

It is the last day of January. We loathe winter and yearn for spring and thus reveal our ignorance and stupidity. For the world is full of mystery now as much as ever. The landscape may look bleak and barren but back of it lies witchery: Nature, the mighty magician, is getting ready for the next spring show. She is assembling her wonders to soon turn them loose, and if we are cunning enough we can spy her at her preparations.

The earth lies fallow and looks drab and uninteresting, but there must be fallowness if there is to be fruit. So it is with us. We have fallow seasons when nothing seems worthwhile. We get nothing done, feel barren and unproductive. Do not despise such times. Learn how to handle the fallow season for it may precede a bountiful harvest. The farmer does not give up in January; he gets ready for August. He knows the desolate season must come and the more desolate the winter, the better the crop. Do we understand as well the tilling of our soul as our soil?

Thus thought I upon my morning ramble.

February 10, 1929

35

A Stroller in Spring

Once more to these hills the miracle of spring has come. Like most good things it does not come suddenly— certainly not on a certain day in March, as the calendars would have us believe. Slowly, a little here and a little there, a bird song and a blossom and a certain flavor in the breeze—that is the subtle path of spring.

A watcher in the hills, worn a bit with the weight of winter, is alert to the very first heraldings of his coming liberation. Better days are in the air, and I am ready to break away from books and typewriter for watercourse and warbler.

The little plum bushes out by the old road have hung out their tiny white banners. To stand in front of them and sniff a western breeze laden with their odors is positively drunkening.

Everywhere, as I stroll, the witchery of a new season fascinates me. The pink of peach blossoms. The red of maple and green of poplar slowly breaking the dull drabness of austere woods. Pussy willows down by the water.

Along with the cheery robin and ethereal bluebird, I consider the flicker of yellow hammer a true John the Baptist of spring. To hear his rolling call on a sunny morning in late March is worth living for. And when away in the woods he drums out a stirring tattoo on a dry, dead limb—that is art and one of the higher satisfactions.

From a distant "hollow" comes the welcome shout of the whippoorwill announcing himself. A vireo broke loose the other day but soon stopped as though he had misjudged the season and sung too soon. The little black-and-white warblers are again circling the trees with their funny imitation of opening and closing a pair of rusty scissors.

Last week a hermit thrush sang ever so softly down in a little ravine near the house. I was preparing a speech for a Rotarian banquet, but when hermit thrushes are singing, speeches can wait, so I abandoned my outlines and attended the concert.

It is a pleasant and fascinating time of year and abounding

in blessing. One's enthusiasm is sobered with the news of storm and death and devastation. Spring has brought that too. The cynical and soured scoff: "Where is there any good? Talk about the glories of Nature! How about a cyclone? That is Nature, too, and not so tempting to the poets! Where is the harmony between crocuses and cyclones?"

We have learned long ago that Nature has another side. She is the mother of both violets and vermin, rambling roses and rattlesnakes. All is not poetry in the woods; there is misery and murder along with the merriment and music.

We do not explain these things. We do accept them as parts of a universe, the goal of which could not be achieved without such a puzzling mixture of bitter and sweet. To all who rapture and dream poetic dreams this is not the ideal. To build character of purpose and integrity is our high mark, and that can not be done in a world where there are no adverse elements.

Why look at the unlovely side? That is negative, and we must live positively to live at all. And we need not forget that without negative there is no positive.

April 7, 1929

36

The Great Outdoors

America is sick today because she has gone indoors.

Yes, the woods were God's first temples, and we have lost much by not worshiping there more today. For all our radios and airplanes, I am not much impressed with the fever of modern progress. I am afraid what we have gained will not justify our loss of this one thing. We have exchanged the glory of the outdoors for stuffy offices and foul apartments and we have reaped a generation of provincial anemics. It was a sad day for the race when somebody discovered ceilings. So long as men are under the blue sky with the music of the birds in their ears and the breeze blowing in their faces, there is tolerance and broad vision. But bring them indoors and they soon start talking inequality, revolution, and Bolshevism. Indoors is the breeding ground of intolerance, disease, and crime. Most of our ever-increasing criminals, suicides, and lunatics might have been saved by a good course of woodcraft.

The average young person can give you plenty of information on football, basketball, and boxing, but what does he know of that far more wonderful world of bird and brook and blossom? He has exchanged the lore of the hills for a load of athletic dope and he is certainly stung on the deal. Baseball is only a little game to be played by people who are not fortunate enough to live in the country, a sort of excuse for not living outdoors. The same is true of other athletics. That they have crowded out the study and practice of woodcraft and outdoor life is a tragedy. It is another witness to the artificiality of a mechanical age.

The Boy Scouts and the Campfire Girls and a few other organizations are heroically trying to preserve something of the love of Nature. We should be thankful that in Theodore Roosevelt we had one president who was alive to the danger of losing our love of the wild and whose great life was a challenge to a softening race. Writers like John Burroughs, Gene Stratton Porter, Thompson Seton, and others have tried to keep the light aglow. But for all that, a boy who would rather go camping than to the World Series is looked upon with suspicion and ridicule. No wonder the love of wild woods is giving way to the love of wild women.

I know that our present economic and industrial world is so arranged that we cannot all dwell under our own vine and fig tree. And I have no scheme by which to give every family a farm and a country home. But I do know that as you take men away from the outdoors and make your cities the mecca of our youth, you are pursuing a policy that has always had unpleasant consequences. Man is enough of an animal that he cannot endure a cage.

When I read of the suicides among our college youth who have found life uninteresting and wearisome, I cannot but wonder. Outside of the world of human nature which is, of course, the highest order of nature, how any man can want to leave a fairyland of birds and trees and stars before he has to is a mystery to me. I'm still enough of a boy that I take that incurable spring itch "when the red, red robin comes bob, bob, bobbin' along." I know the thrill of new violets, the ecstasy of strolling amongst May blossoms, the serene delight of listening in the cathedral of eventide to a woodthrush sing his vespers at the shrine of the setting sun. If you have never sat in the woods "knee-deep in June," as James Whitcomb Riley says, or tramped across snow-blanketed hills, or watched the falling of autumn leaves, or danced in your soul with the daffodils, please don't shoot yourself until you have done that! You will decide then to postpone the shooting indefinitely.

February 13, 1927

37

In the Woods

I am deep in the woods this June day. Nearby is an oven-bird's nest from which the mother has fluttered, feigning injury to divert me from her treasure. Over in the edge of the pines a wood thrush chimes clearly his flutelike serenade. Behind me a hooded warbler, elusive sprite of the underbrush, gaily whistles as if competing with his neighbor, the jaunty yellowthroat.

Overhead a cicada—farmers call him the "dry-weather fly"— rasps his strident summer song. He will not sing long. A few weeks and he has seen his day. But he is not worrying about it. He is making the most of today. So are the ovenbird, thrush, hooded warbler, and yellowthroat. They drink the cup of life as it is passed.

Only we humans "smitten with the plague of thought" take life wearily. Dyspeptic over too much yesterday and hungry for what tomorrow will not bring, we cannot accept the universe and take one day at a time. Yet we boast that we are superior to God's humbler creatures when most of us are little more than animals cursed with worry.

Go to the woods and learn its peace. You are part of all this work and wonder just like the cicada and the yellowthroat. You do not understand this strange puzzle you live amongst, but neither do they. They accept a little of it, abide upon that—and sing. We know enough to live by. Dwelling in the will of God is not a tense, feverish strain; it is a serene, restful thing like the peace of the bird and blossom. They live in His will in their way; why cannot we in ours?

But the cynic pipes up: "Yes, but the bird kills the cicada and the cat eats the bird and nature is a murderous, bloody business. Where is the will of God in all that?" It is the old problem of suffering and evil. We cannot explain it. Neither does the cicada. But he sings! And we humans need not be baffled by pain and death. One lived among us who went through the worst life could give Him and came out on a sunny Easter morning. From the other side of the dark, ugly problem He declares, "He that lives and believes in me shall never die."

Why shouldn't we sing more gaily than the thrush!
So with Sidney Lanier:

As the marsh-hen secretly builds on the watery sod,
Behold, I will build me a nest on the greatness of God:
I will fly to the greatness of God as the marsh-hen flies
In the freedom that fills all the space 'twixt the marsh and the
    skies:
By so many roots as the marsh-grass sends in the sod
I will heartily lay me a hold of the greatness of God:
Oh, like the greatness of God is the greatness within
The range of the marshes, the liberal marshes of Glynn.

And one far greater said: "Behold the birds . . . and consider
the lilies. . . . Take no thought for the morrow for the morrow
shall take thought for the things of itself."
When shall we learn as much of trust and peaceful confidence in the eternal goodness as a cicada and a yellowthroat!

July 13, 1930

38

A Stroller in Snow

All afternoon I have been tramping through the fresh snow. Other things may be headlined in newspapers, but for me a snow is an event of first magnitude.

I went to a spot I call my Pine Temple. And what a harmony of white, green, and blue God has wrought there today! Spotless aisles, softer than any plush; the sturdy columns of the pines, their tops snow-woven into designs only heaven can create; and above it all, the azure sky dome. The prosaic might call it only a patch of pines but it seemed today a snow sanctuary, a cathedral fit for angels.

Out there I dropped the luggage of life's transient trifles and merged for a while back into the elemental world from which I came. It is good for a man to escape to these silences and remember what he is and whence he came. It is not well to stay always amidst the traffic of earth's marketplace, lest in the fever of buying and selling one loses his soul.

Somehow, as I stood in the deep silence of my temple, I felt an unusual kinship with the wonder world around me. Living so much in the tinsel, artificial haunts of men, one feels when he goes into the woods like a returning prodigal—which he is. So it came to me as though a voice spoke it: "You are part of all this. You feel like an intruder because you live so much in the unnatural world men have built that here you seem a stranger. Drop your pack of cares which a silly age has made you think important. Here is your true habitat; stay with us and we will cool your brow and untwist your perspective and help you get in line with God and His universe again."

So I grew calm and rested and cares, like the Arabs, stole away. I listened to the ever-delighted chickadee, the optimist of the winter woods; the jaunty titmouse, and the tiny kinglet, the ruggedest little mite that ever wore feathers; nuthatches exploring head downward, and peaceful snowbirds as serene as the snowy world they love.

Back to a snug chair and warm fire and half-humming those exquisite lines of James Russell Lowell:

> The snow had begun in the gloaming,
> And busily all the night
> Had been heaping field and highway
> With a silence deep and white.
> Every pine and fir and hemlock
> Wore ermine too dear for an earl;
> And the poorest twig on the elm-tree
> Was ridged inch-deep with pearl.

John Greenleaf Whittier's "Snowbound" comes to mind. He little dreamed that his simple picture of a New England home in the setting of a winter landscape would meet instant success, bringing fame and fortune to him in its train. He had struck a chord that reverberates wherever one muses before an open fire, shut in by a snow world outside.

So I came to bedtime with another snow thought finally resting, like a benediction, the sweetest of them all: David's prayer in the immortal Fifty-first Psalm. "Wash me . . . and I shall be whiter than snow" and, as though in reply, the assurance in Isaiah: "Though your sins be as scarlet, they shall be as white as snow."

February 5, 1933

39
Our Modern Nimrods

I have never been a hunter. I have never known the savage delight of lugging a shotgun through the woods and shooting my fellow creatures (and maybe my superiors) just for the fun of seeing them drop. It is a very old and primitive instinct that could be transmuted into better uses and will have to be converted to new purposes within a few more years, as soon as we have finished killing everything. I have spent as much time in the woods as anybody but I somehow get a bigger kick out of just watching the drama of wild life go on than by trying to make a tragedy of it.

There are only two reasons for killing wild things: one is necessity (to procure food), and the other is to exterminate pests. Outside of those two, there is no earthly pretext for a mature man shooting up God's creation. I can't get it into my cranium how a businessman who calls himself a Christian and claims to share Christ's love for all things, great and small, can spend a vacation in the wholesale butchery of birds and harmless animals purely for sport—and then cap the climax by calling it a holiday!

I'm not a sentimentalist either. When I see some podgy old chairwarmer trying to atone for denying himself a natural life by spending a few days out-of-doors murdering up living things for the fun of watching them fall, it isn't a tearful sentiment that I feel. I want to grab a shotgun and go out for big game with two legs and wearing breeches.

Do you know why it is that for every man who loves to stand in the woods and merely watch its pageant of life and beauty pass by, there are a hundred who never tramp the woods except to kill something? It's because most of us are still savages with only a thin veneer of civilization smeared over us. We may be living in a day of radios and new Fords, but when the average man gets outdoors with a shotgun he reverts back in five minutes to his prehistoric ancestors and becomes a brutal savage drunk with a lust for blood.

No wonder the preacher has such a hard time preaching to

the kids on Sundays a religion of love and kindness and gentleness, when on Monday the leading deacon in the outfit (or maybe the preacher himself!) starts out loaded to his ears with cartridges and shells on a mission of plain, unjustifiable murder!

Human nature's a funny old thing anyway. We build up a vast system of poses and camouflages and masks behind which we hide our natural cussedness and call it civilization. We parade around, painted and plumed with artificial pretenses and affectations, and you'd think we were a generation of shining saints. But give the average man a shotgun and a rabbit track, a ticket to a prizefight, or a date with a chorus girl, and he goes back ten thousand years in ten minutes and turns into a lustful savage as primitive as the hairiest caveman who ever hunched in a prehistoric dugout, squinting at the morning sun.

Now they're saying: "Let's junk civilization and be natural." I think we'd better keep on pretending we're better than we are. All progress is a matter of pretense.

But if you're going back to savagery, you'll find no better Moses to lead you than some of our modern small-game Nimrods. They can stand in the presence of God's living creatures and feel in their hearts instead of the thrill of appreciation only the savage lust for annihilation.

December 25, 1927

PART 5

Emotion—The Driving Power

40

Emotional Drunkards

It is customary for us decent folks to roll our eyes and be shocked when some erring brother tucks away a couple of pints of hootch under his shirt and goes on a moonshine spree. But there are other kinds of drunkards besides the red-nosed variety that tanks up on mountain dew and liquid lightning. There are no less than several millions of respectable, well-to-do, upstanding citizens of this U.S.A. who would never think of getting boozedrunk who are drunkards of another type, just as unpleasant and unhealthy and dangerous.

I am talking about emotional drunkards. There are plenty of folks who deplore the plight of the whiskey drunkard who are in a scarcely better predicament. For while he goes off on a rampage from bootleg corn, they fly into a fit of temper or an outburst of hate or a fever of worry or a frenzy of overworked sentiment and enjoy an emotional spree that completely upsets the balance of their lives for days to come. They are completely dominated by their feelings and are run by impulse, not by principle.

Our emotions furnish the driving power of our lives and give life its romance and beauty and pleasure. A person of dull and shallow feeling has a rather dry and barren time of it. But most of us are bothered with too much feeling rather than too little. While our emotions make life rich and full and interesting, they are not supposed to boss the deck. We have intelligence and reason for that purpose and only when our sentiments and impulses are sanely guided and controlled by our minds do we have a wholesome and satisfying experience.

That sounds very trite, and you've heard it a thousand times, but you still get drunk emotionally once in a while. It is a dangerous habit that grows until it sometimes comes to a head in physical breakdown, crime, insanity, or suicide. You may be a deacon and park regularly in the amen corner and be a teetotaler, but if you take a spell occasionally, bawl out your wife, snap at the kids, kick the cat out the door, and then pout like a spoiled child, you're just an old emotional sot, that's all.

We don't control our feelings, and that is the root of all the troubles of mankind. We should become sensibly indignant sometimes but we don't do it sensibly—we have to rave and swear and make asinine exhibits of ourselves. We should be sympathetic and capable of pity, but we overdo it and become silly and slushy and fall into that awful habit of self-pity. We should be happy and cheerful, but we laugh too much at the wrong time and become fools. We should be affectionate and sentimental, but we forget the brakes and stage a petting party when we go to see our girls, whereas we should only kiss them once or twice. We should be religious but we sometimes become fanatical even over that. Poor old human nature has a time of it, trying to keep balanced and sensible, and she is continually lapsing from the straight and narrow way.

But a great deal depends on emotional sobriety just the same. Not that one should become cold and methodical and sacrifice his heart to his head. The great and lovable soul is the fellow whose heart outruns him. Self-control is an art, but it is *heart* and not *act* that furnishes life its deepest satisfactions. Just enough self-mastery to wisely conserve and direct our precious emotions so that we may know the thrills and joys of earth without being devoured by them—that is our need.

The wine of our emotions is given us to make life exhilarating and delightful. But it is up to us to learn how to drink of it without becoming drunkards.

July 10, 1927

41

Education by Association

In every community there is some stupid, awkward, simple Simon who manages to get out into the world for a few years, and then returns home to astonish everybody by using good English and manners so far ahead of his old self that the home-folks wonder, "How knoweth this man letters, having never learned?" And we usually explain it by saying, "Oh, well, he just got out among folks, mixed up with smart people, and picked up better manners." Which sets me thinking.

There are two ways of learning almost anything. Etiquette, for example. You can buy yourself a book on manners and learn all its rules and thereby develop a stilted, artificial code of public behavior that will be starchily evident every time you make your unnatural appearance. Or you may live among cultured people, gradually and unconsciously assume and assimilate good manners, and grow into a gentleman instead of making yourself a gentleman. Of course it's well to mix these two methods, but learning anything by association is by far better than the indirect book way. There is something forced and artificial about the man who has learned his line in a library. You can learn French by studying books, but a better way is to live among the French and learn not only the letter of French but the spirit as well.

If all you learn of any subject is the cold, hard facts, you have not learned it, for you have missed the atmosphere. To study botany is one thing; to tramp the hills and fields and gather flowers, mix with them, make them part of your life is quite another. To be able to play correctly any music placed before you is not to know music. To be able to catch the composer's spirit and message and to give to his notes soul and meaning—that is the mark of the master. And that is not learned by books; it is a matter of heart, not head. It holds true of any subject on earth. The best way to learn a thing is not to study it, analyze it, learn all the rules that govern it. The better way is to forget the rules and get into it with your soul, associate with it, dream of it, inhale the fragrance of it, make it your friend, a privilege to enjoy instead of a task to master. America suffers today from too much analytical criticism and not enough spiritual speculation. That is the seat of all this fuss over the Bible. Too many people use the Good Old Book as a grindstone to sharpen their wits instead of bread to feed their souls.

A lot of this talk about loving Jesus misses the mark because it is misunderstood to mean a sudden outburst of sentiment, which many souls are unable to conjure up, or else it is taken to mean a process to be mastered by study. You can't love Jesus by merely trying nor can you learn how by books. To love anyone demands that the object be lovable, that you be capable of loving, and that association brings you together. Certainly Christ is lovable and any man who has truly found Him has no difficulty in loving Him. There remains, then, this: that you associate with Him, make Him a personal Friend instead of a cold paragon to measure yourself by. Cultivate His friendship by spending time with Him in the Gospels, in prayer, in meditation, in assuming His presence with you in noble endeavor. Learning to love Christ is a process as is any kind of love, but it is achieved through personal, happy association and not by meticulous observance of cold, hard rules. Since you cannot see Him, assume His presence, and in time He will become real.

April 10, 1927

42

There's a Lot in the Hang of Your Head

I've heard and read a lot of verbal rag chewing about the interplay and interrelation of body and mind, how far your dinner affects your disposition, and how much influence your philosophy has on your anatomy. As usual, I haven't learned much but I do think there's a lot in the hang of your head.

I'm not able to tell you just how much power your mental viewpoint has over your appendix, but I do know that the slant of your head is a pretty good index to the state of your heart. You can tell a lot about a man—where he is going and how fast he is getting there—by the way he carries his top piece. In other words the way he is "headed" tells the way he is headed. As the cranium is bent, so is the career inclined.

I know that such a small thing as how you hold your head and shoulders reacts tremendously on your feelings and affects powerfully the way you do things. It may be your feelings that makes your head hang down, but it's also your head that makes your feelings drop down. They react on each other. You rarely see a man who is really getting things done who droops around counting his shoestrings.

Try it out some day when you're all down in the mouth, and the world has jilted you, and you feel like nobody knows the trouble you see. You'll catch yourself with your chin dug into your chest and your shoulders stuck out ahead of the rest of you like the awning in front of a drugstore. No wonder you've got the blues. As long as you go around like you were trying to sneak up on everything, not even a place in Henry Ford's last will and testament could iron the kinks out of you.

Snap out of it. Throw your framework back and set your head up on top where it belongs. Don't try to wear it in front of you; it ain't a headlight! No use being ashamed of it—it's the only one you'll ever have. There may be nothing in it, but throw it back, and stick your chin up and sail right in. You'll feel new power coursing all through you. The thermometer of your spirits will begin to rise, and folks will begin to wonder whether you've fallen in love, inherited a gold mine, or just graduated from a correspondence school in "How to Succeed."

The way you walk outwardly has a lot to do with the way you walk inwardly. Drooping shoulders make a drooping soldier. The guy with a concave chest usually has a concave bank account. It's hard to look up inside when you look down outside.

Life is pretty much the way you take it, after all. If you creep through with a sheepdog countenance, the good things of earth won't come your way. Life's blessings gravitate to the man with his head thrown back.

Don't try to make your chest change places with your back. God made them the way they should go. And He put your head on top. Keep it there.

December 18, 1927

43

Patient Continuance

Those of us who have set out to live in the spirit have sometimes felt discouraged because our sense of the unseen rises and falls and does not maintain one regular, unbroken pitch. We are "sometimes up and sometimes down"; now we are upon the mountain of vision, then we drop into the valley of drabness; now we are high and lifted up, and then life grows insipid and dull.

None of us maintains the various Christian graces at one steady level. Peace and joy, courage and nobility, trust and purity—how we wish we could realize them with an even certainty and fulness all day and every day! But we do not; adverse moods, contrary circumstances, and diverting thought crash in upon us and our consciousness of the eternal is fluctuating and irregular.

There is, however, one Christian characteristic we all may know and hold steadily at all times. The Bible calls it "patient continuance." It means following the Master in season and out, when you feel like and when you don't, obeying the heavenly vision in sunshine and shadow, weal and woe until the race be run.

We gauge ourselves too much by how we feel. Exalted and inspired we imagine we are going well; if we are depressed or sluggish we think we have fallen from grace. But we may be doing a bigger work for God when we carry on and are loyal while we feel hateful and mean than when we preach great sermons or sing loudly in the ecstasy of high emotion. He that endures to the end is saved, and God values more the plodding soul who stays with it patiently day in and out than the excitable brother who indulges in occasional outbursts of rapture.

Some of the graces are of the mind, some of the feelings. Patient continuance is the grace of the will, and a vital and enduring Christian experience centers there. Our sense of faith, of hope, of peace, of joy may rise and fall. But we can patiently continue. When the day is dull, when God seems unreal and heaven far away, we can keep traveling, remembering Billy Sunday's injunction: "Don't throw away your ticket when you reach a tunnel—you'll come out on the other side!"

The true disciple does not always feel blissful and victorious. He is not always deeply God-conscious, but he no more doubts God when moods dim His presence than he disbelieves in the sun when a cloud hides it. Nor does he study a great deal about that side of it. To measure his real condition by how he feels would be depending upon himself instead of God. He patiently continues.

Dark days come and go. Money is lost, goods are taken, health fades, friends forsake or die. Defeat, trouble, gloom, sorrow, weave into life their somber threads of black and gray. But he who has set his face toward the eternal knows that all that is incidental, not fundamental. He knows the sturdy patience of the will is greater than fine thoughts and high feelings. Instead of seeking mental and emotional delights he builds a rugged loyalty to the Christ that will endure when thoughts and feelings grow stupid and dull.

Enjoy the blessings of mind and emotion but make patient continuance central in your experience and all else marginal. Then if the margin be radiant with lofty vision and rapture— well and good; and when it grows pale or dark, the heart of your life still will be intact and enduring.

August 3, 1930

44

In Season, Out of Season

Nothing disturbs some believers more than failure to live continuously upon the mountaintop of high spiritual certainty and inward delight. They are lifted by a sermon or song or prayer or the Word into a veritable seventh heaven. They resolve never again to live the uneven, fitful lives they have known up to now. They start in the spell of a high mood and for a while things go well. But one day there comes the reverse: They get up, physically upset; a sudden adversity lowers the optimism; an unexpected turn catches them off-guard. A sense of things real comes doubly strong: and the fine ecstasy of that other day cannot be captured. And in the midst of a collapse or a drab and dismal mood the poor heart wonders, "Why cannot we be always what we are sometimes!"

As well one might give up farming because all mornings are not ideal, all days not pleasant. Offhand, it might seem a perfect arrangement where birds forever sang and never a cloud spoiled a sunny day. But no one could farm there and soon he would grow desperately tired of perpetual "ideal weather." It is exactly because the seasons are so varied and nature so changeable that we are able to live at all.

The Bible writer tells us: "He that observeth the wind shall not sow; and he that regardeth the clouds shall not reap." It is a world of strangely mixed circumstances and experiences of every sort and shade that we pass through. But the farmer who waits for ideal weather never farms, and the believer who waits for flawless conditions knows no spiritual harvest. While it is not a perfect world, it is adequate for its present purpose; Christian character can be produced here, and that is what we are here for.

Many zealous souls have allowed the Prince of Darkness to sadly spoil their happiness simply through discouragement. Not being able to live at one steady pitch of enthusiasm or to hold regularly to one even degree of experience, they are sorely cast down. And often the trouble is that they have made their minds or feelings paramount, when the whole matter centers in the will.

There will always be mysteries and uncertainties and puzzling problems that the mind cannot fathom. Doubts will assail and apparent contradictions battle in the brain. But we are not saved by what we think but by whom we trust. To be sure, what we think is tremendously important, but even when a man is seriously puzzled over some intellectual difficulty that ought not spoil one moment of his spiritual experience. God's Spirit will lead him to the light if the mind be surrendered to Him. What upsets some who are poorly grounded ought really to strengthen the sinews of the soul, for it is only another step in the growing of a rugged Christian character.

The same is true of feelings. Even Paul did not feel ideally happy all the time. Sometimes he was harassed in mind; again, he was wearied or sick in body; he was no perpetually smiling Pollyanna. But the center of Paul's life never wavered. His will, surrendered with all the rest of him to Christ, never allowed doubt of mind or distraction of feeling to divert him from his heavenly vision. "This one thing I do" he declared, and to Timothy he wrote, "Be instant in season, out of season" because he knew there were all sorts of seasons, and as Peter did on the water, it was so easy to look at circumstance and not to Christ.

This is no tense straining of the will. When Christ possesses the will He keeps it fixed. The trouble comes when we take matters out of His hand and try to handle them ourselves. Leave that center of the life in His hands and puzzles of the mind or moods of the emotions will not spoil your experience. And, as you so live, mind and emotions will fall more and more into harmony with the Christ you have enthroned in your heart.

April 26, 1931

109

45

Jesus and the Blues

John the Baptist was in jail. And he had the blues, which is entirely natural. A rugged, sturdy son of the outdoors, he found a long, rigorous confinement very depressing. He was not at home in a house anyway, and a prison wore down his robust spirit.

He began to wonder about Jesus whom he had so fervently announced as the Lamb of God. Jesus' manner of living was so different from John's. Jesus mingled with the masses, went to feasts, and conducted Himself so differently from the austere ascetic. Was He really that One who should come?

So John sent two of his disciples with the blunt question. We are familiar with the Master's reply. He did not say Yes or No. He merely sent a report of what He was doing. His works were the proof of His claims. By His fruits He might be known. That is always true. A good man need not give his titles and credentials if he is doing things. So Jesus sent practical facts, not lofty claims.

But I am particularly interested in the great tribute Jesus paid the Baptist before the listening crowd. We might have expected Him to reprove the imprisoned prophet for lack of faith, for letting his spirits drop to such a low ebb. Instead He paid him the finest compliments. "John is no reed shaken with the wind, a soft idler cushioned in luxury. He is more than a prophet, he is my forerunner. There has been no greater man born of women."

This is encouraging for you and me. When we are weakest and most despondent, Jesus is most considerate. He did not measure John by a passing mood. He knew his real character which doubt temporarily had obscured as clouds hide the sky. He rates us according to our basic purpose. When there is a break in our progress or we have a spell of depression, He sees the whole of our lives and in the light of that He is long-suffering with discordant details.

If you have the blues and have ever been so harassed at times that you almost wondered whether He is the One who should come, do not be too much cast down. If that is only an incidental mood and not the general condition of your life, Christ will be sympathetic. He is most concerned with the direction in which you habitually are going and not with a spasmodic eruption either good or bad. If your life habitually is away from God, and once in a while you take a good spell, He knows better than that and is not deceived. On the other hand, if regularly you seek to follow Him but sometimes miss the trail He knows better and judges you by your heart's real intention.

It was when John was in his worst light that Jesus put him in the best light. He knows our frame: that we are dust. The bruised reed He will not break and smoking flax He will not quench. If in our innermost being we have set ourselves to know and follow Him and have sincerely and as best we knew how committed unto Him, we have nothing to fear. To be sure, we ought not to have the blues, and as we grow in grace such periods ought to become more and more rare, but many things can throw us temporarily off-key, and we need not let them seriously upset.

Are you temporarily in the jail of a drab mood? Do not doubt the Master, He proves Himself by the things He does. And He knows your heart and will give you His true valuation in spite of perverse temporary depressions.

July 12, 1931

46

The Pose of Poise

Most of us may not appreciate being called unbalanced, but we are. Our lopsided way of living has sent many of us off at a tangent one way or another.

The rarest of creatures is a balanced man. Money or pleasure of learning or society or even religion has upset most of us mortals so that upon one matter or another we are top-heavy.

Of course every man (to achieve anything) must know more about one particular subject than any other. But our common error is that we are likely to think our subject is the only subject there is.

The scarcest of souls is the poised soul. The precious ability to move through the noisy, rack-city marketplaces of earth and not lose one's self in the rabble, that power to pass through the tumult of time and not mistake one segment for the whole— *that* is an unusual thing.

We have everything but poise today. Feverish, restless, frenzied, we fume and fret and tear through our years into nervous troubles. Insanity, suicide, crime, the grave. Or, at best, we are dissatisfied, self-centered, unhappy, and back of it all we are unbalanced. We have no poise.

How shall we get that calm evenness, that smooth harmony that shall turn our discords into delights?

There we err. We think poise is a magical thing to be found suddenly, given for a prayer, discovered in a book. But, like all good things, it does not fall in a lump.

Shakespeare said in *Hamlet:* "Assume a virtue, if you have it not." If you wish poise, this is the order: Assume it, practice it, realize it. For it is an art and must be learned.

Poise is a pose. You have to act it into actuality. You have to begin by adopting the attitude no matter how unreal it may seem. That is the way you achieve anything worth having. The way to become a pianist is to start sitting down at the keyboard, and acting like a real pianist, and keeping it up until you are one.

We have to stimulate anything into reality, that is, above the simple set of instincts we start with. Courtesy, for instance, is acquired and we have to pose it until it becomes natural.

So begin by posing poise. Start today. You may make a mess of it but so do we at the outset of anything. If you've been befuddled and feverish and all out of tune, adopt the pose of poise. If you can hold it through only one or two situations where formerly you flew to pieces you may call it a good day. Just hold to it day by day, and it will become ingrained into you. Almost imperceptibly the new nature will displace the old, and eventually you will discover that you are becoming a new person. What first you have to hold yourself to will become natural. The old nature dies from neglect and the new takes its place.

That is the law of poise. Pose it, practice it, possess it. It is the law of all graces.

One there was who moved through life in perfect balance. Popularity and persecution, pain and pleasure, all the fitful changes of life left His soul untouched. Even upon a cross He kept His poise.

He asks us to be like Him. Rightly does the Book say, "Put on Christ." We must adopt His mind and attitude in preference to our own. We must practice it in every detail of the day. So doing, we become like Him. His nature displaces the old until one may say "For me to live is Christ."

He gives us poise which is peace. "My peace I give, not as the world gives."

Pose it, practice it, possess it.

November 4, 1928

47

Let Your Heart Outrun You

Blessed are the people whose hearts outrun them.

Sitting on our emotions has become a popular fad. Half-baked psychologists and preachers would have us believe that our impulses and feelings are a tribe of dangerous devils to be kept under lock and key.

A strong character or a good Christian means to many minds a pale, anemic mortal who has repressed and depressed and compressed and suppressed his normal longings and desires until he is about as emotional as the Statue of Liberty. Some Bible verses about mortifying the flesh, Oriental asceticism, medieval theology and Puritanic ethics have been rehashed and put out under psychologic labels that really mean: "Your feelings are dangerous; sit on yourself."

There is some sense in it—enough to make it float. Our emotions are dangerous. So is anything that is worth having. They get millions of mortals into all sorts of scrapes every day. But without them life would be about as thrilling as *Butler's Analogy of Religion*, utterly without color, music, fragrance.

So give us the people whose hearts outrun them. They aren't a very safe and secure set. They lead a hair-raising life and keep the staid and fixed souls around them forever on the edge of a nervous breakdown for fear the next caper will wreck the works. They are a little chameleonic and with them consistency is not always a jewel. They are given to fits and starts and rainbow moods, but somehow I like them. I don't care if they do make a break once in a while. They are a sight more interesting than the Pharisees who always do everything right. I'd rather see a hilarious soul whose sensitive strings thrilled gaily even if sometimes not in tune than these drear, dismal human phonographs so "faultily faultless, icily regular, splendidly null."

That's why I'm not a rank critic of modern youth. Goodness knows they've as many faults as Fido has fleas. But they are gamely trying to recover some of the romance their efficient, businesslike elders have thrown out the window in a money-mad standardization spree. Which is worse?

I like folks who tingle with feeling because my Master did. He liked just ordinary mortals with all the usual run of fault and fineness because they had not squeezed out their emotions in an inhuman quest for an erroneous brand of saintliness. He didn't register with the Pharisees; they thought religion increased with the length of one's face. He used a child as His model; and who better than your rollicking youngster lets his heart outrun him!

When the prodigal son—the emotional, impulsive type—got home he got no rousing welcome from that flawless big brother who had behaved himself so carefully. You remember what a lovely disposition that model stay-at-home paraded. And who was the greater sinner?

Of course, idealize your emotional life by spiritual intelligence through the will. But always be considerate of the brother whose feelings have landed him in dutch. Even at that he is a more promising sort that the wooden Indian who has frozen his impulses.

Let your heart outrun you.

May 18, 1930

PART 6

Expectations, Great and Small

48

Don't Ask Too Much of Life

There is such a thing as asking too much of life. Some of us have been too hard to please. We austerely demanded too much of everything and consequently did not even receive enough of anything.

Do not demand too much success. The success magazines and lecturers would have you think that anyone who resolutely spits on his hands and grabs the wheel can steer straight through to a million-dollar job or the president's chair. But success is a strange game; some get there while others as well qualified and as earnest fan out. And those who arrive often find their greatness only a hollow mockery and wish they were back "among those present" again.

Do not ask too much of people. Earth is not heaven and men are not angels. Strange fires are mixed in this human clay, and human nature is not consistent. It is always liable to do the unexpected. Be prepared to be disappointed in the best and surprised in the worst of folks, and do not too easily censure the sons of men. Be tolerant with us mortals—none is so wretched but that in him dwells some spark of good; none so saintly but he may sin. Don't expect too much of mankind.

Don't demand too much of love. The girl of your dreams is not utterly ideal. She is fallible like yourself, and love is no magic wand that will carry you easily through life's tempest and sunshine without a break. Whether you live happily ever afterward will depend greatly on how much old-fashioned patience and tolerance and understanding you weave into your common experience. Don't expect too much of love.

Don't ask too much even of religion. For that is no "Open Sesame" to all life's closed doors and knotty problems—a sort of talisman with which to conjure your way along. While it is born of the spirit and rooted in the mystical, it also is intensely practical and God does not work *for* you so much as *through* you. Religion as a fair and rosy outlook upon life amounts to little save as it is brought down into the daily grind and worked out in the commonplace world. God is no indulgent grandmother to grant the whims of every capricious child; He will go His mile as we go our inch. Don't count on your religion as a sort of soul insurance that looks after your eternal interests, while you go about temporal concerns quite forgetful of it. Religion in a very true sense is what you make it.

In whatever realm you move—career, society, love, religion—do not ask too much of life. Don't be unreasonable; this is not the millennium. Remember you are in the world as it is, and it is a complicated mixture of puzzling lights and shadows that thrills here and disgusts there. Don't worship or condemn too intensely. Mix your enthusiasm with good sense and temper your revulsions with sympathy.

Thus you will not be driven to despair on the one side nor be easily fooled on the other. And if you do not expect too much of life you will not be hopelessly disappointed.

May 11, 1930

49

The Big Parade

I am just an onlooker in the Big Show called *life*. From my house back here in the hills I love to watch the Big Parade go by.

It is a funny old parade, this thing called life. How it started and how it will end, we do not know. Anyway, the show's on, and here are several million curiosities called human beings, swarming around like ants, looking for something—they know not what.

Some think it's *money* and, as William Jennings Bryan used to say, they spend the first half of their lives trying to get everything they can from everybody else, and the last half trying to keep everybody else from getting what they have away from them!

Some think it is *publicity* they need, that happiness lies in headlines. That seems to be the easiest thing out—all you have to do is shoot your wife or start across the Atlantic by air.

Others take the *pleasure* route. They spend their substance in riotous living, and end up with a mouthful of ashes, and learn that pleasure is but another name for pain.

Some turn to *books* and the midnight lamp and look for life through libraries. But of the making of books there is no end, and they wander wearily along with loads of learned lumber in their heads but unable to construct for their tired souls a resting place.

And millions more, bored to death and disillusioned, turn to fanatic fads and isms, perversion and crime, cynicism and despair. Unable to believe that God is now here, they run the two words together and say God is nowhere.

Some cap the climax by suicide. That is too bad. True, I don't know much about this Big Trip I'm on, but I wouldn't stop for anything. You never know what may turn up at the very next bend of the road!

So the Big Parade goes on. What is it all about? Does it mean anything? Do we come from anywhere definite and are we going anywhere for certain? Are we like a squirrel in a cage—plenty of activity but no progress? If life wells up again in the music of Beethoven, full of sound and fury, does it signify absolutely nothing?

From one angle it might seem so. Crime waves. Insanity, suicide, divorce. Political rottenness. Insecurity of our institutions. A formalized, creedalized, money-ized churchanity. It is easy to fly off at a tangent and cry, "Who can show us any good!"

There is another side. Though dark and unpromising at times, this strange process called life wells up again in the music of Beethoven, the genius of Shakespeare, and highest of all, in the life of Jesus Christ. There must be purpose and meaning in the mystery that can produce such as that. I can throw a handful of type into the air a thousand times, but it will never fall so as to form one intelligent sentence. The Sermon on the Mount is not an accident of atoms.

No, life is not a foolish masquerade where the best we can do is to "laugh, clown, laugh." It is a Big Parade, often strange and puzzling, but not a burlesque.

There is an Unseen General in the Big Parade.

November 11, 1928

50

Living the Good Life

The older I become the more I am convinced that only one thing really matters in this hectic mix-up called life.

I have watched the frantic chase of my fellow men for money, goods, pleasure, fame, the tinsel trinkets of earth. For a while I burned with a flaming passion for glory, position, eminence. I have learned that most of the world's fun is not worth the trouble. And in studying this strange little passage called life I have found that the real emphasis belongs to its most neglected line.

One needs only to watch those who have them to know that money and possessions are futile. And they say that money makes one independent! Nothing makes a man more pitifully dependent. The saddest cripples limp around upon golden crutches.

And pleasure—"having a good time"—how vain a thing is that! Vain because we are dependent upon pleasure for pleasure. Take away our fun and we are left disconsolate.

I used to long to be prominent. After watching the prominent awhile I got over most of it. Only a few manage, through a lucky set of circumstances, to get into the Gallery of the Notable. And most of them should be spelled Not Able instead of notable. For every truly great soul who is recognized, a hundred or more just as great or greater pass unknown. The great are not all found out.

Once I aspired to be a great writer. Writing nowadays is a trade, not an art. It is ground out by the yard for syndicates, and one must scribble what the public likes. Of course that makes great writing out of the question. Who can produce a piece every day that is fit for publication?

The original soul will find even the pulpit difficult. The church is highly organized and standardized and a sermon that does not phrase itself in the customary vernacular is viewed with suspicion if not alarm. He in whose name we build our churches would probably not be allowed to preach in most of them.

The man who sets out to live the life worthwhile—to follow his vision and speak his heart—need not look for position, honors, prosperity. The good jobs are sold out to the mediocre. The great die hooted at and are remembered by monuments a century later.

So a sincere soul may be discouraged to find so many roads closed in his face. But the best avenue of all is open to him. He can live the good life. (Nothing prohibits that.) And along that trail lie the only real riches, possessions, pleasures, honors, anyway. What matters it if a silly age overlooks you and there is no demand for your produce in the wrangling marts? If you live the good life, you are rich, great, happy. You enjoy the genuine brand of wealth, pleasure, prominence, while about you men chase the counterfeit.

If you are an honest youth, do not be disillusioned if this world cries for trifles and classics go begging. Stay with the good life. In this befuddled age it provides the only durable satisfaction.

February 19, 1929

51

The Great Illusions

Why do people go to the movies?

Standing on a crowded street, I watched them break away from the passing throng, one at a time, two at a time, and go into the theater. They knew very well that what they had paid for and were going to see was not real, that it was made-up stuff and ground out of a camera. Then why are the theaters crowded?

Simply this: People go to the movies to get away from reality, just for a few moments to be snatched out of actuality to spend in the world of make-believe. We love to get away from things as they are and bathe our souls for a brief while in sweet illusion. Only the eternal can tell how many hungry mortals wander into the movie house because the hard, dull grind of the day by day is almost more than they can bear. They sneak into the theater to freshen their drooping spirits with romance and adventure.

For that reason we read love stories. Perhaps denied in our own lives the loves and thrills we craved most, we drop out of the feverish struggle called living and into a chair. We seek to know vicariously the joy that life has denied us. As we read we imagine ourselves to be the hero or heroine, and thus we live for a few moments through someone else the sort of lives we have craved and never known. Sweet illusion!

We tune in the radio or start up the phonograph or go to hear our favorite music because under its spell we can steal away from things as they are and out into the world of dreams. Charmed by the melodies we love, we can forget for a while that we are farmers and merchants and mechanics, that rent is due, or that we are on a diet, or that we need a bigger salary. We love music because it can drive away reality long enough for us to catch our breath and take a new hold.

So we love to bask in illusion, and in one way or another we seek a few moments respite from the grind of the actual. Some find it in solitude and meditation, when they can sit alone and unfetter their innermost selves. In imagination they enjoy and live those things that they have always pursued and never possessed. Some find it in a favorite game, or a walk, or in prayer, or in the company of friend. And who has not found it most sweetly in the companionship of a sweetheart who understands, with whom he can get away from the fever and worry of business and work and be his own ideal self!

It is well for us if we can retain these sweet illusions—if time and experience tends to brighten them rather than to break them up on the rocks of reality. Happy is the man who can carry with him all the way through this puzzling journey the light of the Spirit and never let it die. It is well if you can pray through and never lose faith in praying; if you can carry your Bible along to the end and the passing years make it sweeter; if you can come down to old age and still find delight in fun and music and make-believe. And fortunate indeed is the man who does not lose the illusions of his courtship. Anyone can get off a fine speech in a swing in June under a mellow moon. But thrice blessed is the man who can look up from unpaid grocery bills with a baby on each arm and his pockets full of paregoric and soothing syrup—and still believe the illusion.

Perhaps the elect will tear their hair over this, but I venture to say it. We go to church because amid the dull, dismal routine of everyday living we hunger for the refining and glorifying touch of atmosphere and illusion. The letter kills, the Spirit gives life—and the letter has pretty nearly killed some of us. Faith—what is it but the substance if things hoped for, the evidence of things not seen—some say, belief in illusion.

When all is said, what is real? The things *we* call real are only the awkward instruments for apprehending and enjoying the ideal. God is the only great and enduring reality.

July 24, 1927

52

The True Art of Putting On

When we see a person acting like something he is not, we usually say, "Aw, he's putting on." In some of its forms pretense is rather disgusting, but although few people know it, one of the greatest aids to successful living is the art of make-believe.

It is not a very good policy to be yourself. For if you lived a thoroughly natural life and acted exactly as you felt, you'd be simply an unrestrained savage and soon be in jail or the grave. Common decency demands that we "put on"; if we were perfectly natural, we'd wear no clothes. We pose a thousand times a day things that we are not, for society requires it. Nobody lives his own life without some camouflage.

This art of make-believe is easily perverted both ways. Some act "good" when they are bad, and the sham in both cases is easily detected. But the secret of real character building lies in living up to your best self, and that is make-believe carried to its highest point. We are all familiar with such terms as "being true to your best moments," "being the man you wish to be," "living up to your ideal self," "living in the Spirit," and so forth. They all mean the same thing: If you wish to be a certain thing, assume that you are that thing and live out the assumption.

If I am a sickly, wretched, fearful, and unsuccessful failure and yet aspire to be a victorious, triumphant soul, there is only one way to it. I must decide what it is I wish to be, mentally assume that attitude, and live every day as though I were what I wish to be until I am what I would be.

This is the secret of the transforming power of vital religion. Paul put it in the very language I am using when he said, "Put on the Lord Jesus Christ and make not provision for the flesh, to fulfill the lusts thereof." That is the verse that changed the whole career of Augustine and made a saint of him. Just put on Christ, mentally assume the character of Christ, and live out the assumption. Imagine that you are Christ and act it out day by day, until it becomes real that you are like Him. There you have the proper use of imagination in religion. Religion has made a great deal of the will but she has always neglected the imagination. Only when imagination and will join hands and work together is great character produced. Too often they work against each other. The imagination creates fears and bogies and mental scarecrows, and the will tries to fight them off, and life wears itself in pitiful, futile tragedy. Imagine that you are what you wish to be! What do you wish to be? A strong character? Then Christ was the greatest character of all time. Instead of aping some abstract mental conception of character, be like Him! Imitate Him, imagine Him, act like Him, and by your will weave your mental assumption into a reality. Simply "put on" His character and live in that attitude and allow no lapses back into your old self. Hold to it rigidly and intensely, and the longer you live like Him the more natural it will become, until you become permanently set in your new nature and the image of the Master is formed in you.

Of course, assume the real Jesus, not the pallid figure of theologies. And remember it is not the literal Christ but His character that you wish to produce. You will retain your own temperament and traits; it is the mind and spirit of the Master working through you that produces the desired character.

However strange it may seem, becoming a real Christian character is simply a matter of mentally assuming the character of Christ and simulating that assumption into reality.

July 3, 1927

53

The Fountain of Youth

Ponce de Leon was not the only one who has sought those magic waters where one may drink and never grow old. We all are questing for that fountain where our spirits (if not our bodies) may be made forever young.

Several years ago, while camping in Florida, I drank from a fountain of youth. Of course I came away even a little older, but it set me thinking of how we dearly pay to drink from this world's false fountains that promise but cannot satisfy.

The fountain of money, of success, of pleasure, of popularity, of knowledge—these leave us as thirsty as before. We press eagerly to the spring, we take deep draughts—but still the body weakens, the mind clouds, the spirit grows frail. These cannot give us perpetual youth.

There is a fountain of eternal youth. The psalmist says of God, "With thee is the fountain of life." Jeremiah declares that the people "have forsaken me [God] the fountain of living waters, and hewed them out cisterns, broken cisterns, that can hold no water." How lamentably true today!

Long ago, Jesus sat by a well where a woman had come for water. He told her of a water of life which He had to give. "Whosoever drinks of this water you are after will thirst again but whosoever drinks of the water that I shall give him shall never thirst." *There* is the fountain of youth. We drink of it when we share the eternal life of God through Christ. It does not preserve the body for the outer man decays, but as we live upon it the inner man grows younger day by day.

This is no mere exalted euphony, born of a high mood. They who share the God life through Christ have perpetual youth, which is another way of saying eternal life. In spirit they grow younger instead of older, for they share the life of God. Their bodies are only the little shells that life temporarily uses.

When Jesus used a little child as the type of His true disciple, I believe He had this in mind. The Christian has the spirit of eternal youth. Where did we ever get the gloomy notion that a believer should creep about with a face like a landlord's conscience? He should be as joyous and hilarious as a child, for he is the only youth who never shall grow old. Only children and the childlike are genuine—all others are clowns.

I am sure that we never have caught this thought of eternal youth in our religious life. We have always identified the spiritual with a serious look and a grave decorum as though Christ called us to a funeral instead of to a feast. When the prodigal returned home he found music and dancing. More prodigals might return to the Father's house if we made a more gladsome thing of it and did not have so many sulking, Pharasaic older brothers on the backporch.

Jesus said something more to the woman at the well. Not only will those who drink of this living water never thirst again, but "the water that I shall give him shall be in him a well of water springing up into everlasting life." We ourselves become fountains of youth sharing its spirit and overflowing its blessings wherever we go. Others find in us that spiritual youthfulness they have been looking for; they long to drink as we do from our hidden springs; they take knowledge of us that we have been with Jesus.

Let us leave these broken cisterns and drink of the eternal waters!

February 22, 1931

54

Where Is Your Joy?

We all are seeking more joy in one form or another. The money chaser, the businessman bent over his desk, the prodigal at a wild party, the traveling vacationist—all are seeking a greater degree of joy or happiness.

But not many have joy for all their ardent quest. Most of them are looking for a different degree of joy when what they need is a different kind. How many worried faces one sees nowadays upon the streets! The lined and painted faces tell a tale of disillusionment. The newspapers eloquently declare in their columns of crime, suicide, insanity, cynicism, the sad story of a joyless world.

Most of us are expecting joy from wrong sources. First of all, it does not lie in *where you are.* It is not a creation of circumstance. Poor human nature persists in thinking the next field will be greener. A new house, a new car, a change of jobs, a trip—forever just ahead lies happiness! When we are "well fixed" we shall have joy, we think. But we are never well fixed unless, like the psalmist, our heart is fixed (57:7). No, joy does not consist in where we are. If we are not happy here, we shall not be there.

Nor does joy consist in *how you are,* that is, in how you feel. Feelings are as variable as April weather and a joy based upon mere emotion is at the mercy of a headache or a bad dinner. God's Word speaks of a joy that can exist with suffering. "Ye became followers of us, and of the Lord, having received the word in much affliction with joy of the Holy Ghost" (1 Thess. 1:6). Christ tells us we shall have trouble, then bids us be of good cheer (John 16:33). True joy is deeper than how we feel.

It is not a matter of *who you are.* Position and prominence do not bring joy. Men seek fame and high places only to learn that they were happier in obscurity. The secret of real joy has been kept from the wise and prudent and revealed unto babes (Matt. 11:25).

Neither is joy dependent upon *what you are*—your own character. Many are deceived here. Nicodemus and the rich young ruler were men of fine character but they still sought something deeper; they had not found true joy. Our own goodness may bring us a sort of self-satisfaction but it never sparkles with heavenly joy for it is hollow—a sounding brass and tinkling cymbal.

Where then is true joy? It consists in *whose we are.* Jesus Christ is the source of joy and only as we are His do we find His joy. The Gospel is a message of joy, the very word meaning "good news." The Lord Jesus spoke again and again of His joy (John 15:11; 16:22, 24; 17:13). The New Testament proclaims it (Acts 13:52; Rom. 14:17; Gal. 5:22). Our Lord said, "Be of good cheer; it is I; be not afraid" (Matt. 14:27). It is the "I," our Savior and Lord, who makes the difference between fear and cheer. Someone has said: "Joy is spelled *J* for Jesus, *O* for others, *Y* for yourself; put Christ first, others next, yourself last." Others have spelled it to mean *J* for Jesus, *Y* for yourself and *O* for naught, nothing between you and Jesus.

If we believe, then we are Christ's (1 Cor. 3:23)—and in whose we are, we find joy.

May 6, 1934

55

The Security of the Saints

Are you afraid of dying? Are you one of those neurotics who move from one symptom to another—forever dreading sickness? Does a pain in the chest give you visions of a sanatorium, an ache in the stomach suggest operations and hospitals? How many poor mortals go through life, a thermometer in their mouths, fingers on the pulse, hastening to the doctor with every little pain!

Once I thought I had tuberculosis. I had disturbing symptoms, night sweats, pain in the chest, loss of weight. I had examinations at this clinic and that, until my money was gone. I lay awake nights worrying, painting dismal pictures of a "lunger's" fate. There were miserably morbid spells when impenetrable darkness seemed to settle with no hopeful ray.

One day I began to wake up to the folly of such a course. I knew that I was the Lord's and He was mine, that no harm could come to me on ocean or on shore. My little old body might break and disintegrate but my real life was hid with Christ in God. Theoretically I had been believing that for years; now would be a good time to live up to it.

So I left my burden with God. I got outdoors, took sunbaths, ate plenty of food, lived simply, calmly. And my troubles of body and mind fled away.

I think often of Paul's verse "Whether we live, we live unto the Lord; and whether we die, we die unto the Lord; whether we live therefore, or die, we are the Lord's." It reminds us of another passage of his where he was in a strait between two desires, to depart and be with Christ, and on the other hand, to stay on earth and labor. And the secret of it all is "To me to live is Christ, and to die is gain." I like to think of Paul here as standing upon some lofty eminence where, no matter which way he looked, he saw Jesus only. To live was good, to die was good; no matter what came it was good, for since he was in Christ all things worked together for good. If he lived it was unto God; if he died it was unto God. There were no more dreads, fears, horrors, for his life was hid with Christ in God.

There is a divine carelessness, a heavenly indifference to earth's shifting circumstances and conditions that delivers us from all our nagging worries and feverish fears. Many of us, theoretically, have been trusting the Lord for years, but practically, we have been trying to hold ourselves up by our own bootstraps; we are in a nervous strain and tension that is breaking us. We shall have relief and peace when we realize that, living or dying, we are His and turning loose our strenuous grasp relax upon the everlasting arms.

A friend of mine tells me that he lay in agony of body and mind in a hospital, when in the midst of a particularly miserable spell it seemed that a voice spoke to him, "Be still and know that I am God." It set him to thinking: *Here I lie making myself sicker. The doctors have done their best and I have done what I could; why worry further? Be still and let God do what He will.* He told me that he went to sleep and from that moment began to get well.

Blessed state of the believer when he learns to practice what he claims to believe; that, living or dying, he is the Lord's! Come sickness, disaster, whatever may, neither powers nor principalities, life nor death, things present or to come, can separate him from the love of God. Sink of swim, live or die, succeed or fail, obscure or famous, abounding or in want, nothing can affect our standing in Him. For our life is hid where circumstances cannot find it, hid with Christ, hid in God.

September 13, 1936

56

You Can't Pay Your Way

One of the great delusions of the natural man is the idea that he can work his way to heaven. How many times have we asked people about their hope of heaven, and they have answered, "I'm trying to get there. I'm working that way," and similar replies which indicate that they expect good works to land them within the celestial portals.

But no man can do enough good works to go to heaven. We do good works on our way to heaven and because we are going to heaven but not in order to go to heaven. Jesus Christ purchased our ticket with His own blood and no extra fare is required. By grace are we saved through faith and not of works lest any man should boast (Eph. 2:8, 9). "Not by works of righteousness which we have done, but according to his mercy he saved us, by the washing of regeneration, and renewing of the Holy Ghost" (Titus 3:5). "To him that worketh not, but believeth on him that justifieth the ungodly, his faith is counted for righteousness" (Rom. 4:5).

Of course, this is distasteful to the natural man. He likes to think that he can do something to save himself, to merit God's favor. But it is just as we are without one plea but that His blood was shed for us.

There is a greater danger here than first appears. Plenty of people in our churches today mistake church work for that good works which proceed from union with Christ and to which we are created in Christ Jesus. They work for the church earnestly and faithfully, just as they work at other times for some other organization and feel that by such labors they are making down payments on future salvation. But much of it turns out to be loyalty to their local church, to put it across, and ahead of other churches in town, and their work does not proceed from a saving relation to Christ. In the Book of Revelation, chapter 3, the church at Sardis had a name to be alive but was dead. Here evidently was a very active church for it had a reputation to be alive, but it was really dead, for its activity did not proceed from Christ and was dead works instead of living fruit.

We need a rediscovery of what the grace of God is. We need to learn that eternal life is a gift from a loving God to an undeserving race of sinners—a gift made possible by Christ's death—and that we don't earn gifts; we either take them or refuse them. Then our works do not in any wise contribute to our salvation; they are the expression of our new relationship to God. We do good deeds because we have been saved and want to see others saved.

Such a viewpoint knocks out all the props of pride and allows no flesh to glory in God's presence. Our modern church activity is based too much on recognition of human effort and gives too much credit to ourselves. We have learned to glory too much in how many demons are cast out and not that our names are written in heaven.

There is absolutely nothing we can do about our salvation except to realize that we can do nothing about it, save to acknowledge ourselves lost and accept the gracious pardon God offers us through Christ. Then we shall engage in good works by way of thanking Him for His grace.

March 12, 1939

57

A Day of Disillusionment

It is a day of disillusionment, of fallen castles, and faded dreams. Men set out expecting too much of life, and the outcome is dolefully evident in literature of pessimism; in the prevalent cynicism of "Oh, yeah?" and "What's the use?"; in divorce and dissipation and the increasing suicides. Our forefathers lived in meagerness and hardship far poorer than the plainest moderns; but they found life eminently worthwhile and had no time for the weird perversions of this petted, pampered race of neurotics. Life was real, life was earnest, and the grave was not the goal.

Prosperity has a habit of spoiling and rottening human integrity, and it has played havoc with us today. So soft and thin-skinned and faint-hearted have we become that a depression that would have been child's play to the stout hearts of our ancestors has terrified us into hysterics.

The root cause of human disillusionment is a warped approach to this matter of living. We expect too much of life and expect too little of God. To live sturdily, abundantly, satisfyingly, one must learn not to count heavily upon life but to depend utterly upon God.

To expect much of life is soon disconcerting. We gather money and possessions, and the treasures that looked charming enough at a distance seem paltry when they are ours. We quest for fame and earthly honors only to learn that the higher we climb, the more plainly people can see us, and we long for obscurity again. We interpret life in terms of "eat, drink, and be merry" and soon we are left, bitterest of all, with tortured nerves and a mouthful of ashes. We love, we marry, we build up a home, when in stalks calamity and heartache and death—and one day we are sitting upon an empty hearth again. We form friendships but the dearest hearts are severed, and life is the more desolate for their passing.

Life is too fickle, too nakedly open to the inroads of change and circumstances to be a secure basis for satisfaction. What thrills us today will sicken us tomorrow, and the fairest treasure we hold can so easily be swept away overnight. It is foolish to promise a man an unbroken string of delights if he will be good. The old saints were under no idle delusions about life. They knew that the world is not friendly, and that he who lives godly must know sorrow and heartache.

Expecting great things of God is another matter. Move up from the folly of counting heavily upon life and learn to depend upon Him. There is no disillusionment there. The same old shifts of change and circumstance will come but they cannot devastate your soul. It is not what actually happens to us that matters so much as the way we were looking at things when they happened. The man who expects too much of life is wrapped up in incidentals, and when things go wrong so does he. But the soul that is grounded upon the eternal knows that all things work together for good. If money is lost, that is not his true treasure anyway; if he never becomes famous he knows that what matters is what God thinks of him. If home is broken and dear ones lost, he knows they can meet again. It is a wonderful life that "is hid with Christ in God."

Don't expect too much of life, for life is tricky, undependable. Expect *everything* of God. He is the one permanency in a changing world.

> Change and decay in all around I see;
> O Thou who changest not, abide with me.

December 13, 1931

58

Help Answer Your Prayer

Nothing has been more grievously misunderstood than praying. Many a well-meaning soul has besought heaven for strength of character, power of will, a vigorous spirit, and a victorious life and has totally ignored one fundamental element of prayer without which no such petitions ever can be answered.

We must help answer our prayers. We ask God to do things *to* us which He must do *through* us.

There is a very significant distinction. A sturdy character, holiness of life, triumphant faith, are not kept in heaven like goods in a store to be dispensed to whoever calls at the counter of prayer, freely handed out for the asking. While in a sense they are obtainments, they are also attainments and are secured through the cooperative grace of God and hard work of man.

God does for no man what the man can do for himself. Many an earnest soul has zealously prayed for years to no avail and has grown disheartened because he wanted done to him what only could be done through him.

To be sure our part is small. But God can not go His mile until we go our inch. Someone has said that a farmer expends only 5 percent of the energy required to grow a crop; the forces of nature supply the rest as the farmer cooperates. But suppose the farmer decided that since his part was so negligible he would leave the farm to nature!

Our part in the growing of character may be as small as that but it is indispensable if the forces of the spirit are to be worked into the texture of a worthy life. And to pray for victorious living without cooperating with God for it is as ridiculous as a farmer praying from his front porch for a rich harvest while the plow rusts in the field.

The very nature of prayer makes it easily liable to abuse. It is so much easier to ask for things than it is to get out and help bring them to pass. But God would do us an injustice and harm to make character a matter of asking instead of achieving.

The parent who gives his child every request without teaching the child to help make some of his desires real is laying up trouble for the youngster later on. God is no coddling grandmother; in a very significant sense He helps those who help themselves.

Prayer is no magic "Open, Sesame" before which every door easily flies open; prayer is a man getting in touch with God for a cooperative undertaking.

Strength to master evil is developed in practice. No athlete ever acquired his strength merely by praying in a gymnasium. The sinews of the soul grow rugged by exercise. Prayer has its tremendous place, and without it our straining is largely in vain, but it never can supplant the practical part we play.

Don't ask God to do to you what He must do through you. Help answer your prayer.

August 24, 1930

PART 7

Heeding the Inner Voice

59

Dad Blodgett—An Obscure Celebrity

It was late one evening when I arrived in the village which I am going to call Willow Vale. After supper I reclined comfortably on the front porch of the one and only inn, and having disposed of the weather and other generalities, asked the innkeeper, who was smoking his pipe beside me, a pertinent question.

"Tell me," I ventured, "of your acquaintances here, past and present, what man has been the greatest asset, of the greatest value, to this community?"

His reply was prompt. "Dad Blodgett, without a doubt. And I think all the villagers will agree with me. And the remarkable thing about it is, he wasn't wealthy, never held any office, nor did he leave a handsome bequest for a public park or a monument. But his monuments are walking all over this place, and he left a fortune that they can't compute down at the bank."

This was interesting. I asked for more.

My host refilled his pipe. "Well, Dad Blodgett lived here all of his seventy-one years, except when he was induced to take a pleasure trip to Washington. He went up there, listened to the senate one day, and was never known to discuss politics afterward. He owned five acres of land, kept the post office and a few groceries. His big, old-fashioned house beside the store used to be the center of Willow Vale. The best way to tell you what sort of a man he was is to tell it indirectly. Whenever we had any little squabbles around here amongst the neighbors, we always went around to Dad Blodgett's instead of going to law. He knocked Squire Simpson out of many a case. When Bob Wilkins's wife died, and he was so wrought up, he went around to Dad's every night for a month to get cheered up. When Jack Surratt got mixed up in that forgery mess he went straight to Dad's to talk his troubles.

The young folks gathered there at least once a week, and the youngest one in the crowd was Blodgett. He wasn't bewailing forever these hell-bent youngsters. Oh, he'd get hold of one if he learned he was going crooked, and when Dad got through with him, he felt like two dimes, but Dad always had faith in youth. We used to go there when we'd lost some of our folks, after the funeral, or when some of the kids would go off to school; it was so lonesome, you know. I don't know how he managed it, but he was always lending books to the school kids and giving garden stuff to a dozen or so poor families. The boys ate up his cherries and apples, and the girls took his flowers, and he loaned hundreds of dollars he never got back, but it always seemed the more he gave, the more he had.

There's Squire Simpson, prosperous and high standing, but he's always lived for himself and he's no asset. And we've got a doctor, two preachers, and a community worker, but the whole kit and caboodle can't come up to Dad. I think he was such an uplifter because he didn't make a business of it. When folks find out it's your profession they get shy."

I went around to Dad Blodgett's home next day. I saw his old favorite Bible. And on the fly leaf he had written this verse: "The world passeth away and the lust thereof; but he that doeth the will of God abideth forever."

August 14, 1927

143

60

Living Like Jesus

Charles M. Sheldon wrote a book some years ago called *In His Steps*, in which he tells the story of a church that really undertook to live like Jesus. It is deplorable that such experiments have been largely confined to storybooks.

Men have speculated much on what would happen if an individual or group would actually set out to apply Christianity to every detail of life, to subject every issue with which they dealt to the test: *What would Jesus do?* While we build churches and pay preachers and observe the outward forms of religion, most of us prefer to let George do the practicing it. Except for isolated tryouts, real Christianity doesn't get much exercise.

I can conceive of no greater, more romantic and interesting adventure than to undertake to live like Jesus in this complicated day. Of course a thousand puzzling questions would arise. It would be interesting to know how a man so minded would handle such issues as evolution, politics, the League of Nations, Al Smith, the movies, modern flappers, big athletics, and prohibition. One thing is clear however: Jesus did not lay down minute rules to cover every little problem. Had He done that He would soon have been out of date.

In His own day Jesus met specific problems with general principles as in the money and marriage questions. Had he formulated precepts to govern every little issue, his religion would only have been a sublimated form of legalism. It is His spirit rather than His teachings that we need most in solving our difficulties, and the man who tries to live like Jesus will subject each matter to the test of Jesus' spirit rather than His words. He will put the spiritual attitude of Jesus foremost. The intellectual side of each problem he will tackle from the viewpoint expressed in the teachings of Jesus. But he will not make of his religion a set of regulations. Christianity is the infusion of a new spirit, not a system of laws and by-laws.

But, anyway, wouldn't it be a glorious adventure to start out to live like Jesus! I know a man who says of his clothes,

"These are not my clothes; they belong to Jesus. I keep them in good shape that I may not hinder my message by a slovenly appearance." That sounds eccentric and cranky to us sensible folks, but it is like Paul, who gloried in being so wholly devoted to Jesus that the world classed him crazy. We have grown so respectable and circumspect that we have lost the romance of religion—so afraid are we that Mrs. Thingumdoodle across the street will talk about us at the next Tattling Circle. Suppose every Christian storekeeper would say, "This is not my store, it belongs to Jesus and I am only His clerk"; suppose every farmer would say, "This is Jesus' farm and I am only His tenant." Suppose every Christian took that attitude. It would be entirely correct and Christian, and if they really lived out such an attitude, you' d see things happen. Those early disciples in the Acts didn't rate high on the social and cultural calendar. We Baptists and Methodists and Presbyterians who glory in our influence and numbers could learn a lesson from some of the smaller sects. They may not be up with us in scholarship, but some of them have recovered wonderfully the radiance and simplicity of the early church.

It is often said that if the church would really practice its religion, the world would soon be converted. It would not. The world would turn on the church and persecute it as before, for the church would upset the playhouses of profiteers and infuriate the Pharisees and run modern money changers out of the temple. A serious application of Christianity would revolutionize the whole order of things and the church would suffer many things. But men would learn that the religion of Jesus can really do things—that it is not a matter of new moons and Sabbaths but an adventurous, revolutionary and daring way of life. There would be some contrast between it and the way of the world. And it would make some progress, for Christianity thrives best under opposition.

March 13, 1927

145

61

"Don't Let Nobody Turn You 'Round!"

A few Sundays ago I preached at a black church. I asked the congregation to sing for me an old-time spiritual, and they broke loose on "I Shall Not Be Moved!" I won't forget that song soon, sung as it was with such simple but mountain-moving fervor. I carried away from that meeting this conviction: In this fast, feverish, jazzy age, what we need most is spiritual permanence, the enduring ruggedness of soul that will not let us be moved.

The big word nowadays is *change*. Everything is changing, some for good, some for the worse. Change is one of the laws of progress. But there are some things that don't change. And in an age when people are so dominated by impulse and mood rather than principle, we need a few stalwart souls whose hearts are fixed, who cannot be swayed by every wind of doctrine.

We have plenty of genius, wit, and beauty, but real and abiding characters are scarce. People with backbones instead of wishbones, people whose defense is inside, not outside, are few and far between. But one of them is worth all the syco-phants and sissies who parade in men's clothes and are nothing but the slaves of their own whims and feelings and the spirit of their time.

The black people have another song along that line: "Don't Let Nobody Turn You 'Round." Most of us are easily turned around. Money, fun, popularity, feelings, environment, and associates get us excited and make fools of us. Happy is the man who can move through the turmoil of today, keep his own counsel, his head clear, his soul clean.

> Do what thy manhood bids thee do, from
>   none but self expect applause;
> He noblest lives and noblest dies who makes
>   and keeps his self-made laws.
>   Sir Richard Francis Burton

I like these substantial characters who don't let things turn them 'round. That's what fascinates me so with the Master of

Galilee. Popularity couldn't puff Him up. The consciousness He felt of His own powers didn't overbalance Him. The bitterness of the Pharisees, the hostility of the scribes, the stupidity of His disciples, the violence of the mob couldn't turn Him from His way. It was a hard way and it led to Calvary's lone gray hill, but nobody ever turned Him 'round.

It takes something to live like that. It takes hours of solitude and prayer and you have to keep a room in your heart sacred to God and let nothing intrude upon its holy privacy. When friends forsake you and enemies grow vicious, you have to run back into that little room, recharge your soul, and rekindle your vision. It takes sacrifice and self-control and discipline and devotion to stern duty and a lot of similar things that have gone entirely out of style nowadays. It takes high thinking and clever living and a willingness to be cussed and laughed at and called weird for the sake of the integrity of your life. Oh, it's no snap, the way is straight and narrow and few there be that travel it.

But the old high road is wonderful and glorious for all that. The climate is clean, the air is fresh, and at the close of each day you can sleep with a clear conscience and the feeling that you are not ashamed to look at yourself in the mirror when you get up. It is a steep and rugged trail, but there are vistas along it that repay the climb a thousandfold, wide ranges of vision that the merrymakers down in the valley can never know.

And, best of all, at the end of the old high road is God.

July 31, 1927

147

62

"Trust and Obey"

For many years I prayed for visions and special revelations in my spiritual experience. I heard and read of spectacular instances where puzzled souls were suddenly given certainty by divine interventions as amazing as the fleece of Gideon. I craved such supernatural illumination for myself, but though I sought it earnestly, it never came.

I longed for some sort of inoculation of my spirit with power from on high that might make me forever immune against the fevers and poisons of sin. I wanted suddenly to be transformed with a transfusion from God that would guarantee me against mistakes and keep me always just as I should be. But I never have been miraculously lifted out of the fight for character nor does my spiritual makeup run along without jar or friction.

But the years have taught me something better. Instead of looking for God to step in and handle my business, I have learned to trust and obey.

If every matter I am uncertain about were worked out like a mathematical problem and handed to me in a dream, I would walk by sight instead of faith. I would need no faith and all the adventure would be taken out of my life, leaving only a tedious routine.

If I were suddenly changed into a full-grown Christian character as by a magic wand, I would not remain so. For the very struggle and persistence of striving after goodness through the years is what knits together the integrity of a sturdy soul.

So now I trust and obey. I do not ask for sign of fleece or magic answers to my problems. Yet His grace is sufficient for me, and as I travel along, the way grows clear and looking back shows me that wisdom greater than my own has had in mind the journey. I do not know or understand much in the universe around me; only the present I see and both ends fade out of my sight. But I think the threads come from somewhere and go somewhere and that God holds them in His hand. I trust.

I try to obey. I want to live my best according to the light I have today. I may learn more tomorrow that will make what I did today seem erratic or even wrong. But if I did my best according to my light I shall not grieve. I obey awkwardly, stupidly, sometimes maybe sullenly, for I am not always an ecstatic soul. But the Master liked better the boy who said, "I go not," yet went, than the other boy with the fine emotions who didn't go.

I like the old verse, "Trust in the LORD and do good; so shalt thou dwell in the land, and verily thou shalt be fed." Trust and do good—that is my program. There is nothing high-sounding about it; but it is all that we can do. And when a man has done that through the years he knows there is enough packed in those four words to keep every moment filled with thought and action.

> Trust and obey for there's no other way
> To be happy in Jesus but to trust and obey.

October 26, 1930

63

The Inner Light

Often we have heard people say that this or that thing is not wrong because it is not condemned anywhere in the Bible. Preachers frequently are consulted on problems of amusement or conduct as though somewhere we had a list of every detail of human thought and activity drawn up in two columns, the good and bad, and properly checked up by the Almighty.

The Bible is not a chart of what we may or may not do. The object of the Book and its Christ is not to furnish detailed information but rather a new spirit and point of view. A Christian lives, ideally, from God's point of view as revealed in Christ as he best understands it.

A real Christian has a different outlook upon everything from the rest of folks because he views the temporal in the light of the eternal. From that standpoint, things that look big to others dwindle, and what others rate trifles become momentous matters. If the Christian does not rave over worldly amusements and interests it is not because he is a gloomy Puritan in the straitjacket of a code of blue laws; it is rather that he has found a higher range of enthusiasms that so eclipses these trivialities that they lose their charm.

When problems of conduct do come up, the believer does not refer to an itemized list of the right and wrong procedures. Jesus did not sit about passing judgment on minute matters of thought and behavior. Rather, He gave us principles which, when illumined by His Spirit, cover all situations. The Christian pleases to do right, then does as he pleases. With him, the attitude is: "What would Jesus do in this case? Does this make for more abundant living? Is this in tune with God's eternal point of view as I understand it?" While one's judgment and understanding may be faulty, and while more light later on may revise some of our decisions, certainly this is the only course for a Christian. As he yields more and more to the inner voice of the Spirit, his own judgment becomes more and more in tune with the Infinite and puzzles clear up as he meets them because the Light within shows them up in their true perspective.

If one is in doubt, he had better not do the thing until he is certain. If something has to be done he can only breathe a prayer for guidance and meet the situation with the light he has. If he acts up to his best light, he has done no wrong in God's sight, even if his action itself was not ideal. Still, he must not idle along depending upon what light he has but rather by study and meditation and prayer increase his light. If he does not continually strive for more light, then he is not justified in living up to the light he did not try to increase.

There are also situations where the act in question is not wrong in itself for one to do, but its effect upon others will be evil. There one must keep in mind the other fellow and limit his own liberty for the sake of the greatest good. But if the other fellow makes a business of taking offense at others, he does not deserve such consideration. There is a difference between the weaker brother and the faultfinder who looks for flaws.

Amid the maze of all such problems one thing is certain: Christ drew up no regulations; He sought rather to give us His spirit and mind and point of view. The Pharisee lives by meticulous observance of rules and laws. The Christian carries his law in his heart. One is the love of law; the other is the law of love.

December 21, 1930

64

"Thy Will Be Done"

Many times we have repeated that petition in our devotions with scant understanding of what it really means. The Lord's Prayer used to be the standard finish to chapel exercises in countless schools; it is glibly recited in all sorts of services, many of which our Lord might never endorse. Most of us know it, we think, "by heart." And that is exactly the way we do not know it.

For if this model prayer were in our hearts instead of merely in our heads, we would be seriously careful when its profound petitions crossed our lips. A man had better be careful how he prays, "Forgive us our trespasses as we forgive those who trespass against us," for if he does not forgive those who wrong him, he is inviting upon himself a curse.

But I am thinking just now of that portion which says, "Thy will be done." For one thing, the man who asks that and does nothing to help realize God's will on earth is a rank hypocrite.

But think of the two sides of this petition. Most of us see only one side, that of resignation. When inevitable trouble or mishap comes along, when adversity that we can neither avert nor help breaks upon us, we drop our heads upon our breasts and say, "Thy will be done." That is a true Christian attitude and blessed is the soul who can so meet such hours. In our Gethsemanes when the path of duty means for us a cross, our prayer should be His: "Not my will, but thine, be done."

But there is another side. Praying that God's will be done is something more than resignation to adversity. There is an aggressive note in it. Doing God's will on earth means a bitter struggle with the power of evil: strongholds must be destroyed, sin condemned, judgment declared, the wicked reproved, fortresses of vice and corruption must be attacked, wicked practices uprooted, crooked conditions straightened, dens of darkness and iniquity invaded in the name of the Prince of Light. That is aggressive business and in that sense we need tremendously to pray, "Thy will be done," and then go forth into the fray to help make our prayer come true.

Unless one sees both sides of this prayer, resignation and aggressiveness, he will do some one-sided praying. And there is no more flagrant hypocrisy abroad in the land than the superficial repetition of these stupendous words, unsupported by surrendered wills and lives. Verily, we call Him Lord but do not His commands.

Do not forget the war cry in this prayer. There is more in it than pious acquiescence to the inevitable. "Thy will be done" means: May evil habits and practices be swept from my personal life; may my home life be above reproach; may my business activities be carried on in the mind of Christ; may my social conduct be transformed, not conformed; may I stand in all public relationships for Christian principles, the kingdom of God first; may I stand in the church for the gospel against all forms of false doctrine and reveal an active faith through practical works done through the Spirit and not merely my own ability. A man is calling for a big order when he prays, "Thy will be done."

Truly this is the prayer of the bowed head, for when the clouds lower and circumstances beyond our power to affect hedge us about, it is time to pray "Thy will be done." But it is also the prayer of the raised head, the head thrown bravely back as one goes forth in His name to meet the foe and fight the good fight; there, again, we may truly pray, "Thy will be done!"

April 5, 1931

153

65

Are You Putting the Christ in Christmas?

Christmas morning. Presents and fun and excitement. Presently you will go to church—maybe. You will hear the cantatas; the minister will preach his Christmas special. There will be a big dinner and a day of mirth and merriment and that is well.

But how many of you will remember what it is all about? Will you leave the Christ out of Christmas?

Some of you are good, respectable, church folk. Your name has been on the roll these many years, and you are always in your pew Sundays. You respect Jesus, you are expecting Him to save you, you sing about Him, pray to Him, pay the preacher to tell about Him—and let us hope he does instead of weaving pleasant homilies on popular topics. But how real is Jesus to you this morning? Is He close at hand, as Tennyson wrote: "nearer than breathing, closer than hands or feet," or is He a distant abstraction almost in a class with fairies and Santa Claus?

What does He mean to you? Are you actually seeking to live His way, or do you plug along by your own wits and will? Is He but a figure of the church having, so far as your experience goes, no kinship with reality? Are you proudly living your own life, "the master of your fate, the captain of your soul," or can you truly say with Paul, "To me to live is Christ!"

The worst of all unfaithfulness to Jesus is that which pays Him deference and courtesy but does not His will. It is so much easier to honor Him with our lips and pay him churchly homage than to let Him have His way in our lives. Men say nice things about Him today. Lecturers pay Him tribute, moralizers use His truths to point the moral and adorn the tale. Thousands of fine people would never dare utter a word against Him. But does He not see through our tawdry pretense and does not His Word still hold true; "Why call ye me, Lord, Lord, and do not the things which I say?"

Once there was a young merchant who was anxious to rise in his work. He also liked to play checkers, which is not evil except when it gets in the way of something better. One day he was playing a game with a friend in his store when a rather shabby looking stranger dropped in. The merchant made one of those mistakes that is not uncommon; he asked the customer to wait just a moment until he had finished the game. Then the stranger bought some small article and went out. Next day a neighbor asked the merchant: "Do you know who that customer was? He was the manager of a chain of stores and was looking for someone to take charge of one he plans to set up in this community. But, he told someone that although you had been recommended he could not risk a man who would let a customer wait until he finished a game."

Jesus is passing by and He calls on you. Will you let Him wait until you have finished your little game? "Not now, Jesus, but when I am older and have had my fun. When trouble comes or death threatens, when I have done things my way first, at some more convenient season, I will deal with you." Do not be surprised if the Great Manager passes on. He cannot dwell where He is shunted aside for trivialities. To be sure, life's lighter issues have their place but it is not first place. "Seek ye first the kingdom of God, and his righteousness, and all these things shall be added unto you."

This Christmas, do not be so preoccupied with the checkers or lesser things that you forget the Customer from Above. He has not come to stop your mirth and merriment; He only wishes to exalt you to better service that greater joy may be yours.

Are you putting the Christ in Christmas?

December 25, 1932

66

Resting for God

Of resting in God we have heard much. But do we rightly appraise the value of resting *for* God?

As we read through the Gospels we keep coming across such instances as this: Jesus has had a wonderful day of teaching and healing. Multitudes crowd about Him, hang upon His words, astounded at His works. Then suddenly He escapes from it all to ride across the little sea or retreats to a solitary place to pray.

We might not have done that. Carried away with our own success—drunken with our achievements—we might have pressed on through the night and so overdone things. We might not have withdrawn from such admiring throngs at the very height of popularity. But Jesus knew the value of resting for God.

It is as imperative to rest as to work. That holds true in things spiritual as well as elsewhere. Sometimes one can do more for God by doing less. To keep driving at high-pressure, overtaxing body and mind, is to do only mediocre work. Better work less and do that excellently than be forever busy with indifferent results. Keeping everlastingly at it brings only high blood pressure.

Employers have found that better work can be secured from men working shorter hours. A man's work is in proportion to his rest. Many an overzealous preacher has done little by trying to do too much. He has been too much a Martha in the kitchen and has neglected to "choose that good part" in restful attention at the feet of the Lord. We really do wrong when we are more concerned with the quantity of our work than with its quality. Many an overworked Christian would best glorify his Lord with a camping trip of healthful relaxation. It is well to be still and know that He is God in a fresh reorientation of the soul away in some mountain cabin or by a riverside.

Jesus was not in a hurry. He knew the world could not be changed in a day and He simply sowed the seed and knew that God would attend to the harvest. How finely balanced He kept

His life! He never let the whirl of popularity, the excitement of His work, even His own zeal for the tremendous things He must get done in three short years, carry Him to extremes. There was always time for a rest in the solitudes, a boat ride, a fishing trip. He knew how to rest for God.

How much we need to learn that lesson in these feverish, frantic days. Life is too much for us as it is lived now. The nervous frenzy of these hurrying times is taking terrific toll in insanity, suicide, physical, mental, and spiritual exhaustion. We must learn to be still for God though we have to renounce fond interests and be counted old-fashioned to do it. After all, we Christians are called to be separated folk, transformed, not conformed. We must simplify our schedules though it means leaving out some perfectly good, Christian details. Multiplicity means mediocrity. We shall do better things by doing fewer.

And when we rest, let us not be impatient about it. We are serving the Lord just as much when we truly rest for Him as when we work for Him. "They that wait upon the LORD shall renew their strength."

March 26, 1933

67

The Unshelved Life

A great many people are living confused and wretched lives today because they are like stores without shelves, and with the goods scattered indiscriminately all over the floor.

Every man should arrange his life and shelve his interests as a man would stock a store. There is a shelf for fun and one for work and one for study. There is a place for exercise and one for business and one for recreation. There is a corner for good books and music, and one for sporting the girls, and one for prayer, and one for his home. If he has a hobby, an avocation, let him fix quarters for that; if he is a radio fan he should make room for that; and if he loves to fish or go hunting let him space off a section for that. All the interests, enthusiasms, and concerns of his life should be fitted into their respective places as orderly as a man would arrange his wares in his shop.

But we don't do that. We mix up our enthusiasms in a hopeless hodgepodge with little things often on top and big ones buried beneath, and we live disordered and purposeless lives. Or else we become so interested in one concern that we ignore all the rest and become lopsided and unbalanced—if not actually crazy. We spend all our time at the radio shelf or the work shelf or the study or amusement shelf, and part of us withers and dies while the other becomes abnormal. We become so enthusiastic over tennis, or sporting the girls, or arguing Scripture, or making money, that soon we have only one shelf, and we are about as serviceable as a store with one shelf. There is no life that can endure continual concentration on one thing. There must be variety and diversion and change to keep us refreshed and balanced.

Jesus lived a life of many enthusiasms. He loved to be alone in the solitude of the outdoors. He also loved to mingle with people in daily living and share with them their sorrows and joys. He went to social festivities as well as to church. He knew times of anger, spells of depression, moments of sublime inspiration, and hours of grief. He touched life at all points and his storehouse was stocked with many interests. But He was the manager, He didn't let his interests manage Him. He kept every detail of life where it belonged and allowed no single item to crowd out others. And He left us that timely injunction, "Seek ye first the kingdom of God and his righteousness; and all these things shall be added unto you." In other words He reminded us that each man is a storekeeper but that his store belongs to God, not to himself. Keep your store with that in mind and seek first of all to please the manager before you please the clerk. And if you have, at the last day, been faithful in a few things you shall be promoted to a higher position.

Keep your storehouse in order. Don't work all the time lest you become a grind. Don't play all the time lest you lose all integrity and become a parasite. Don't allow any mood or interest to crowd out the rest and take up too much room. Do what you do with all your power while you're at it, but don't stay at it all the time. Live a varied life with time to play and pray, work and worship, dream and do.

Does your store have shelves? Or are the goods scattered on the floor? Or is it a one-shelf store?

May 29, 1927

68

Mendelssohn and the Master

In the cathedral at Freiburg there was a wonderful organ. One day a man entered and asked the custodian if he might play upon the great instrument. The old keeper finally granted permission, grudgingly.

The stranger sat down and slowly began to play. The attention of the old sexton was arrested; he dropped into a seat and listened spellbound; soon tears coursed down his wrinkled face. He had never heard such music before.

The stranger arose to go, and the custodian followed him silently to the door. Finally he managed to ask, "Who are you?" The visitor answered simply, "I am Mendelssohn." And all that the old man could do was to throw up his hands and cry, "And to think I almost refused to let you play the organ!"

Every man is the custodian of the organ of his soul. What pitiful discords we make when we try to play our own instruments unaided, try to live our own lives by our own strength. Everywhere worn faces, weary hearts, broken spirits tell the story; the custodian cannot play his own organ.

But One who is greater than Mendelssohn asks to sit at the keyboard of your heart. He will bring forth music from it that you never dreamed could be there—melody instead of melancholy, hallelujahs instead of heartaches. Not only will it thrill you but others will be drawn to hear for they will perceive that you have quit playing and that the Master plays instead.

> Down in the human heart,
> Crushed by the tempter,
> Feelings lie buried that grace can restore;
> Touched by a loving heart,
> Wakened by kindness,
> Chords that are broken will vibrate once more.

Doubly true is that when His heart and hand take us in charge!

I think of the rich young man who came to Jesus. What a magnificent keyboard of possibilities he carried! But he chose

160

to be his own musician and went away sorrowful "for he had great possessions." But of what use is an organ if it cannot be played, and of what use is a life abounding in promise if we deny Him who alone can make anything of it?

Jesus is passing by. Through the ages He has been bringing heavenly harmony from even the most unsightly organs. Who else could have made anything of Simon Peter? What a harsh instrument was Saul of Tarsus! Think of Augustine, the slave of lust; what an unpromising prospect was Moody, the shoe salesman; what melody could be expected of Gipsy Smith?

Mind you, we never were meant to be the organists of our souls. We cannot play but we are the custodians; we can let Jesus play or refuse Him. All the trouble in human lives begins when the custodian tries to be organist. The playing is God's part; the permission is ours.

August 23, 1936

69

How to Abide Forever

Only one thing really matters in this world—to live in the will of God.

We are cumbered with many things—money, possessions, making a name, earning a living. We fret and fume, get hot and excited, fight and argue, about a thousand trifles that would be laughable could we view this feverish fuss of living from another world. We sweat and strain for that which satisfieth not and the fruit of our labor is not worth the cost. We call ourselves efficient, but the average mortal is continually cheating himself from cradle to grave.

And but one thing is needful if only we know it—to live in the will of God.

Everybody with good sense believes in God. Atheism is only a mild form of insanity. He has a purpose for these little lives of ours as well as for the collective universe. The sum total of life's real meaning is this: Get into this will of God and live there.

Then if you have tuned in with this infinite keynote, you have solved the puzzle of existence and you are ready for whatever comes. You no longer live for money, for you have learned what a pitiful thing it is and what little it can buy. You use it but you are under no delusions; you know where your real treasures are.

You know that your property is only yours in name to use while you stay here. Soon it will pass back out of your hands into the general sum of creation; it never was yours; you are only a steward. So if you lose it all you are not bereft; how can a man be bereft of what never was his?

Health may fail, but you know that you are more than body; that is only the little machine you run about in. Friends may die, but you have not truly lost them and you do not grieve as those who have no hope. You may be obscure and despised, but you are interested in character, not reputation, and your kingdom is not of this world, so you are not enamored of its silly standards. Come what may, earth-shifting circumstances are but passing ripples on the boundless eternal sea. Your real life is beyond any of the things that happen.

It is a blessed thing to live in the will of God. One who does that is God's ideal man, for He said of David, "I have found a man . . . after mine own heart, which shall fulfil all my will." To do His will is our sustenance while we are here, for Jesus said, "My meat is to do the will of him that sent me." Our society is composed of those who do His will, for Jesus said, "For whosoever shall do the will of God is my brother, and my sister, and mother." Our prayer while here is "Thy will be done." Our promise is, "If we ask anything according to his will, he heareth us." And our prospect is, "He that doeth the will of God abideth for ever."

How is it done? Jesus is the highest expression of the will of God, for He is God's mind and Spirit lived out in human life. Therefore, accept Him. Make Him your ideal. Share His Spirit and life, and by God's help through faith set out to look at life and live it as you honestly believe He would.

And your life shall pass from its pitiful discord to the tuneful harmony of those whose "life is hid with Christ in God."

March 8, 1931

PART 8

The Judgment to Come

70

Listening to Yourself

I have just returned to my retreat among the Pasquotank cypresses from Philadelphia where I preached Sunday for the radio preacher, Donald Grey Barnhouse. An interesting incident connected with the services was that my sermons were recorded on phonograph records as I preached them. After I had finished preaching, I went into another room and heard myself all over again.

Which set me thinking of how each of us is recording a life, and one day we must hear it over. My childhood impression of a recording angel setting down every move I made may have been exaggerated in some particulars, but the principle of it is true. *We are being recorded.* The Bible declaration that every vain and idle word must be accounted for ought to sober our careless walk and talk.

In preaching these sermons I had to be careful for defects of enunciation, clearing of the throat—everything was reproduced. Yet we move thoughtlessly through these years beneath the eternal eye and ear and forget that one day our little story will pass in review before us. For the things we think and do are boomerangs—they will return.

The man who claimed such echoes in his mountains that at bedtime he could shout from his window, "Wake up!" and the echo would come back next morning to rouse him was certainly lying, but life is full of its echoes. The things we shout upon the hills of youth will return in later years to please or plague us. You cannot escape it. Chickens come home to roost, and bread cast upon the waters will return after many days. The record is being made, and eventually we must hear ourselves.

Our lives are making their impressions in more ways than we imagine: upon *ourselves,* so that in later years we often are but the scratched and jarring record of earlier sins and excesses; upon *our children,* so that in them we relive our own careers; upon *our community* which, if we have served it truly, will always be a glad witness reproducing the good we left behind us.

Often I think of the tremendous record made by Dwight L. Moody. Over all the world one continually runs into lives he touched, institutions he inspired, movements he set going. And each is a record repeating and amplifying that first impression, though the man long since has gone to his reward.

Many of us have phonograph records of Caruso. He is dead, but his voice sings on and so, being dead, he yet speaketh. In a greater sense death merely shifts the lever, and all we have been and thought and done comes back in the lives and recollections of those who knew us, in letters we wrote, in deeds we did. In uncounted ways we come back.

Be careful. In old age you must hear the record of youth. At judgment the life passes in review. And the ripple you start will undulate on to eternity's farthest shore. No life that ever was set in motion has ever ceased. It goes on in its far-flung influences somewhere.

It is a sobering thought and in the light of it "what manner of persons ought ye to be!" How careful we are when we learn that a few words will be taken down and will be heard again at will. Yet how thoughtless often we are in thought and deed, when every move is cutting its place in the record of time. How we ought so to live that we might not be ashamed when our record is played!

May 15, 1932

71

Men and Trees

Much interesting truth in God's Word gathers around trees. In the Garden of Eden were the Tree of Life and the Tree of the Knowledge of Good and Evil. Man is shut out from the Tree of Life, and we go clear through the Bible before we reach it again in the paradise of God in Revelation. That is true in more ways than one; we must go all the way by Calvary to reach the tree we lost in Genesis. The way to the garden of God from the garden we lost through sin lies through another garden, Gethsemane, but the Lord has traveled the road for us.

In Genesis we find a man behind a tree. Adam hiding from the Lord after his sin. How men seek to hide today behind this excuse and that, behind arguments which often seem plausible, when the real trouble is that they are sinners and dread His presence. There is no tree that can hide you from Him. When He calls "Where art thou?" you must stand before Him naked and ashamed.

In John 1:48 we find a man under a tree—Nathanael under the fig tree in prayer and devotion. Instead of hiding behind the tree, the place for us is beneath the tree in repentance and prayer. We like to parade this silly excuse and that, but the truth is, it is "not my brother nor my sister but it's me, O Lord, standing in the need of prayer."

In Luke 19:4–6 we find a man up a tree, Zacchaeus looking for Jesus. If you earnestly, anxiously are seeking Him along the roads He travels He soon will bid you come down from your sycamore, for He must abide at your house. Then, like Zacchaeus, come down and receive Him gladly into your heart and home.

All this is possible because of One upon a tree. It was Jesus "Who his own self bare our sins in his own body on the tree, that we, being dead to sins should live unto righteousness." Galatians 3:13 tells us: "Christ hath redeemed us from the curse of the law, being made a curse for us: for it is written, Cursed is every one that hangeth on a tree." Back of all the mystery of the atonement, the at-one-ment of God and man through Calvary, lies the simple fact that Christ died for us, and there is hope for us only at the foot of the cross.

I used to hear the old preachers pray, "Hide us behind the cross" and wondered what they meant. I have just spoken of Adam trying to hide behind the trees in the garden. There is only one tree that can hide us from Him and that is the tree of the cross.

Revelation 6:16 pictures the unprepared crying to the rocks and mountains. "Fall on us, and hide us from the face of him that sitteth on the throne, and from the wrath of the Lamb." They are trying, like Adam, to hide from His presence. Then I read in Psalm 31:20; "Thou shalt hide them in the secret of thy presence." The best way to hide from God's presence is to hide *in* His presence. We can hide from Him as Judge by hiding in Him as Savior and Father. Rocks and mountains cannot conceal us but our lives may be "hid with Christ in God" (Col. 3:3).

There is one other tree I wish to get under. That is the tree of Revelation 22:1–5 in the City of God with its twelve manner of fruits and its leaves for the healing of the nations. I belong to a race which, by eating of one tree, lost its right to the Tree of Life. I cannot hide behind any other tree save the cross. I must get under the tree of prayer, like Nathanael, and up the tree looking for Jesus, like Zacchaeus, and down from it at His Word. If I come to His cross, hide behind it, glory in it, I shall have a right to the Tree of Life in the City of God.

June 12, 1932

72

Brawn, Brains, Bible

Through the course of history men have tried to live by three creeds, the creed of brawn, the creed of brains, the creed of the Bible.

The creed of *brawn*—that might makes right—has been given a long tryout through centuries of war and woe. It has been tested from the days of club and javelin on to this age when Nietzsche and Prussian General Friedrich Bernhardi and German General Paul von Hindenburg undertook to realize it afresh at the cost of world misery. It has by no means been discarded for its ugly head rises threateningly today amidst gigantic armaments and deep-laid schemes for world dominion. It can never prevail for the meek shall inherit the earth, and the Lamb shall triumph. Men have sneeringly said that the only way the meek will get the earth will be by inheriting it, but God has decreed that brute force must fail. It has failed so far as the ruins of Babylon and Rome, the story of Saint Helena and the exile at Doorn attest. Might is not right.

Men have also pinned their faith upon *brains*. Knowledge is power, they declare. So it is, but what kind of power depends upon who exercises it. Education changes size but not sort. The most dangerous man is an educated bad man. Men pride themselves upon their inventions, but it is sadly evident that most of our machines turn out more evil than good because the machinist is wrong at heart. We have built a Babel with our science and the end is confusion of tongues.

For instance, men's brains are set at present upon eliminating war. Writer and political analyst Alexander Powell, a man with world experience, speaks revealingly when he says: "The real causes [of war] are injustice, oppression, jealousy, greed, hatred, suspicion, fear. I have no patience with disarmament conferences, naval parleys, bickerings of professional diplomats, and politicians, the futile fiddling of the League of Nations. They are not striving to cut out the canker itself. They are merely and half-heartedly putting salve upon the sore" (*Liberty* magazine, March 7, 1931).

It would be an amusing thing if it were not such a sad picture of our diplomats conferring here and there, trying by human wisdom to meet a problem that only a change of the human heart ever can master.

The other creed is the way of the Bible. When one mentions that, there is a tendency among many to smile tolerantly and say, "Oh, yes, the Bible is quite all right but then, of course, we can hardly make it practical in such a world. The Bible is for church; we are looking for a practical solution that we can work out here and now."

Of course, we do not expect the Bible to appeal to those with whom it has become only an interesting collection of ancient writings for critics to debate over. Nor is the Book a guide as to how we may solve humanity's problems by our own strength. It is a revelation of God's plan and purpose in history and it shows how we may find a place in His plan so He may work through us. God is going to solve the puzzle of life; we never can; but we can enter partnership with Him.

It is not by strength nor by smartness but by His Spirit that we prevail. And through the revelation in His Book lies the way to life in His Spirit.

June 21, 1931

73

A Word to the Grouches

There is one pet sin which most people seem to think the Lord does not ask us to give up. Everybody will agree that drunkenness, immorality, lying, and thieving are terrible; that hypocrisy may be worse; that crookedness in business and profanity and slander are reprehensible. But almost everybody will make out a plea for plain, old-fashioned grumpiness. "That's just my nature," they explain. So we have those miserable souls who are guilty of none of the sins mentioned above, who are respectable citizens, and loyal church members, but who are a thousand times more difficult to live with than some who do the more deplorable things.

I wonder whether we have any worse sinners than those irritable, peevish mortals who get up each morning with a disposition like a cross-cut saw; who move through the day as though all the world were out of step except themselves; whose faces are as though all the family had died the day before. Pity the people who have to live amongst such human gloom factories with a countenance like a landlord's conscience and a disposition so sour it must have been born in crabapple time and put up in vinegar!

To say that it is one's nature to be so is absurd. Certainly no Christian has any right to such a plea, for he has passed from the old nature to the new, and there is no place in the Christ nature for such sour demeanor. To say, "But when I do 'fly up,' it's all over in a minute" is ridiculous. All over in a minute? So is a shotgun. And how dyspepsia does get the blame for what is due the devil!

"But if you were in my circumstances . . ." pipes another grouch. Christians are not regulated by circumstances. "All things work together for good" to them. They profess to believe their Bibles and then moan about their "condition." If our lives are hid with Christ in God that is our true condition. The trouble is, we look at God through our circumstances, instead of looking at our circumstances through the light of God.

I do not know of any harder place to live the spiritual life than in a home infested by one or more grouches. There will be a fine reward for the husband who kept his tongue and stayed calm whilst he lived out his days with a rasping wife. "A continual dropping in a very rainy day and a contentious woman are alike" (Prov. 27:15). The same holds true with the woman whose wedding may have been among orange blossoms but who has lived with a lemon.

I hear many sermons on obedience to parents but not yet have I heard anything about Colossians 3:21, "Fathers, provoke not your children to anger, lest they be discouraged." Part of the blame for many rebellious children and discordant homes goes to a parent whose disposition is a continual provocation to lose one's temper. Woe to those contrary mortals who will go any length just to be hateful! Ours is a terrific responsibility along these lines. We shall give account for our churlishness. Do you make it easier for people to be good while you are around? Or, do you forever rub fur the wrong way and make it easier for everybody to lose their good nature and spoil the day? I had as soon be guilty of some of the less respectable sins as to be a professional grouch.

Wake up, old sourface! God does not give us any special permit for grumpiness. Rather, love is the ideal. And "[Love] suffereth long and is kind."

October 18, 1931

74

The Prosperity Bunk

We Americans have been reminded so often lately about how prosperous and increased with goods we are, until we are pretty well fed up on this opulence balderdash. Orators have waxed eloquent upon it, lecturers have dilated thereon, platformists and inkslingers have used it for a steady text, while the Republican party has sought to epitomize its past two administrations in the key word: *prosperity*. And pointers-with-pride of both parties are declaiming, "We must be the greatest people on earth. See how rich we are!"

We may be prosperous for all I know. If we are swimming in wealth, I don't know it. Over where I live there is still plenty of dry land. If I belong to the richest crowd on earth, it certainly is doing me personally the least good of anything I know. America may be flooded with dollars, but they don't come my way.

But they tell me we are prosperous, so I'll agree just to be sociable. Suppose we are prosperous? I wonder if that is anything to brag about. "To have is to owe, not own" and we should take it seriously as a sacred trust and responsibility instead of something to crow about.

Our financial status is no index to our true condition. "Rich" is so often followed by "rotten." The most suitable text for us Americans at present is the old Bible indictment: "Thou sayest, I am rich, and increased with goods, and have need of nothing; and knowest not that thou art wretched and miserable and poor, and blind and naked." We are afflicted with Laodiceanism.

> Ill fares the land, to hastening ills a prey,
> Where wealth accumulates, and men decay.
> Oliver Goldsmith

It is one thing to have great material possessions; it is another thing to know how to use them. If we really are prosperous (although investigation may show that most of the prosperity belongs to a few profiteers) that is well enough in its place. But if we do not have the spirit and brains to rightly handle what we have, then we are accursed instead of blessed.

The very thing we are bragging about is probably the worst trouble we have. We are raving about assets that may be liabilities.

I am not impressed by wealth. I wish somebody could think of something better to say about the U.S.A. than merely that she is prosperous. Our wealth is getting us nowhere. It is making the world jealous and resentful, and Uncle Sam has changed from the Big Brother to the Big Bother. Our money may be leading us into fearful poverty ahead.

Unless our spiritual and moral wealth keeps pace with our financial gains, the devil will be to pay. Our prosperity has gone to our head. Something must sober this jazz-mad land. It is no time to talk of how well fixed we are. It is time to notice what a dangerous fix we are in.

Is the young generation prepared to administer this fabulous wealth? Are we piling up carfare to hell for our successors? Our real problem is not prosperity but posterity.

The prosperity line is being overworked. Will somebody please think of something else?

December 23, 1928

75

Not Many Noble

The country has been swept with an epidemic of bigness. The standard has been size instead of sort. I am growing tired of big men. Our big men have brought us into the dumps we are in now. We need some good, ordinary men. The superman of this high-powered age has failed to show up. Mass production has not been accompanied by man production. We have built a machine too big for the mechanic. One does not have to be a technocrat to see that.

"When Earth's last picture is painted, and the tubes are all twisted and dried," the really big men will rise from the ranks of the obscure: country preachers who labored for years, maybe with unappreciative congregations; country grocers who kept up half the community by credit bills while the chain stores got the cash; country doctors—no specialist ever will take the place of the old country physician who knew everybody by the first name and was a human being, not a professional automation. Experts and specialists of all sorts have run us ragged. Someone has described a specialist as one who knows more and more about less and less!

Jesus spent little time hobnobbing with the elite and the upper crust. He went among common, prosaic people doing good. He said once in prayer; "I thank thee, O Father, Lord of heaven and earth, because thou hast hid these things from the wise and prudent, and hast revealed them unto babes" (Matt. 11:25). Again, He said: "Many will say to me in that day, Lord, Lord, have we not prophesied in thy name? . . . and in thy name done many wonderful works? And then will I profess unto them, I never knew you: depart from me, ye that work iniquity" (7:22, 23). He rewards at judgment those who fed the hungry, took in the stranger, clothed the naked, visited the sick and imprisoned (25:35, 36).

Christianity began among the poor and despised classes and never suffered a harder blow than when Constantine made it fashionable. Paul, perhaps with his rebuff from the Athenian smart alecks in mind, writes to the Corinthians:

For ye see your calling, brethren, how that not many wise men after the flesh, not many mighty, not many noble, are called: But God hath chosen the foolish things of the world to confound the wise; and God hath chosen the weak things of the world to confound the things which are mighty; And base things of the world, and things which are despised, hath God chosen, yea, and things which are not, to bring to nought things that are; That no flesh should glory in his presence (1 Cor. 1:26–29).

Forgetting that, churches and denominations plunged into sprees of competition for the most numbers, the biggest churches, the most impressive figures. "Statisticitis" swept Protestantism like the flu. Now all are hard put to it to save their faces. Like the builders of Babel, we undertook to "make us a name" and the end is confusion of tongues.

If we spent less time trying to make a hit with the Athenians of the modern Areopagus and got back to the Corinthian simplicity, we should fare better. Most of the notable turn out to be the not-able. God's greatest truths still belong to babes.

February 19, 1933

76

"I'll Get By"

One hears it everywhere nowadays—"I'll get by."

"I'll skim over my studies and cram for the finals and manage to pass. Who wants to be a valedictorian nowadays anyhow! Just so I get by." "I'll sneak this pint in the backseat and look the cop in the eye—and I'll get by." "I'll tell the wife I was detained at the office and take her a present—and I'll get by." "I'll shoot him and drop him in the river—and I'll get by."

So it goes from small issues to the momentous. What is the leading business in America? *Getting by.* A sophisticated generation that thinks it can outwit the eternal is at it from the little to the great playing with fire and gambling with death, and sober souls who would warn or caution meet that defiant little "I'll get by."

Most likely those who play that game will lay this little piece aside with a casual yawn but for all that, we humbly remind you that nobody ever gets by.

Getting by is simply one of those things that never has been and never will be. The man who tries to get by is bucking a fundamental law of life that is a little too deep to get under, too high and wide to get over or around.

One may get by in school and barely pass by the skin of his teeth. All the rest of his life he'll pay the price for a superficial education that is not solid and thorough enough to meet life's demands.

One may get by the officer with a pint, but he usually tries a quart next, and so on, straight into jail. And if he never gets caught by any cop, the unseen policemen of God's changeless law will jail him in a far worse prison than that of brick and stone.

One may get by unsuspecting customers and cheat his way to a handsome profit, but he pays for it with a cheap and tawdry soul. Always the cheater is finally cheated. Bigger scales than his weigh him up, and he is found wanting.

One may hide his unfaithfulness and impurity from his own

wife and friends, but in one way or another the dirty truth leaks out, and deep down in his heart he carries a living hell.

One may, once in a long while, cover up the grossest crime. Sometimes the murderer stays at large, but he carries along a picture of a dying man to rack forever his soul with misery worse than the punishment of law.

And worse than all this, another world lies beyond where all the loose ends of this tangled and unfair world are straightened out, and every man gets his due. *No one gets by there.*

Of all fools the get-by crowd gets the ribbon. They play a game that they never win, for across the table sits the Master Cheat, Satan, and we poor saps are not in his class.

"I'll get by." But you won't. The Detective of the Universe is on your track, the sleuths of God have an eye on you. They never lose a man. Somewhere you come to court.

You can't get by.

December 29, 1929

77

God's Cure for Disappointment

Is there anything that wears down the human spirit more than the bitter grind of disappointment? Whether in such small ways as looking for a letter that never arrives or in such major matters as the failure of life plans, the cup of disappointment is a sure test of character. How many lives end in cynicism, bitter failure or suicide because the load of shattered hopes was too heavy to bear!

God has a sure antidote for disappointment. It is that simple faith that finds expression in the dear old Bible verse: "We know that all things work together for good to them that love God, to them who are the called according to his purpose."

If we Christians really believed and lived out this grand old verse we never would be plagued with worry and vexation. Here is the recipe for the carefree life.

Of course it has its conditions. We must be sure that we are among those to whom this assurance applies. It holds good only for those who love God and are the called according to His purpose.

"Called according to his purpose" does not mean that God arbitrarily selects some and rejects others. The next verse explains that God called those whom He foreknew. God, foreseeing that some will choose Christ, predestinates them. God elects those who are candidates for eternal life. If we have accepted Jesus and trust Him we are the called and elected.

To love God (the other qualification) is not a sickly emotionalism but that devotion of the soul to God that puts Him first and ever craves fuller knowledge of Him. The wife who loves most is not always the one who is most emotionally affectionate, but rather she who proves her love by a life of loyalty and devotion. It is so with the believer and God.

If you belong to those who are the called and who love God then utterly commit all you are and have into His keeping. Do your part of course as well as you know to help all things work together for good. A man cannot neglect his health and then in sickness bring up this verse in justification. Such sickness is not the good working of God's purpose but the consequence of his own wrong living. But if you have honestly lived in His will up to your best light and are fully trusting Him, then you need never be disappointed, no matter what life may bring. All things—not *some* things but *all* things, even the most commonplace and grievous things—work together for good. Incidents and circumstances that seem to have no possible connection are threads in the great tapestry of His purpose. And one day when life's little fevers are past, we shall see the whole design and marvel at the way He wove together the tangled strands of our ragged lives to serve His purpose.

And all things work together for good. Not "for the best that could be done under the circumstances," not just "somehow or other," but definitely for *good*. Sometimes we say of a sick person, "He took a turn for the worse." No Christian living in this verse ever takes a turn for the worse. Even death is for the better, for as Paul put it, that means to depart and be with Christ.

A marvelous recipe for the conquest of care! And it was not written by an armchair philosopher idly fitting together fine sentences at a summer resort. It was penned by a worn, old preacher whose life had been a stormy round of hardship, heartache, prisons, beatings, persecution, and pain. It worked for him and certainly ought to for the rest of us.

September 13, 1931

PART 9

In Times of Testing

78

The Tasteless Hours

One of the problems of this little experience called *living* is, What shall we do with the tedious and tasteless hours?

Did you ever have a day when everything went wrong; when your blood ran lazily and your mind went on a vacation and your whole disposition was so sluggish and dull and dead that nothing looked good to you, and you didn't even care whether you lived or died? You simply couldn't stir up the least enthusiasm for anything; nothing excited your interest; no challenge could wake your lethargic soul? We have all known such days, and most of us don't master them, they master us.

Many causes produce these stupid days. Sometimes it's the weather. Or a sluggish liver. Sometimes the devil and sometimes dyspepsia. Maybe overworked nerves and we need a vacation. Or just plain cussedness. Bad habits of thinking. Sometimes it's because we need salvation and sometimes because we need Sal Hepatica. Anyway, they come.

Not long ago I had such an afternoon. I tried a walk in the woods, but Nature held no charms. I tried to read, but the printed page could not attract me. I played the piano, but it was tinny and soulless.

And then there flashed into my mind that dear old Bible verse: "They that wait upon the LORD shall renew their strength; they shall mount up with wings as eagles; they shall run, and not be weary; and they shall walk, and not faint."

That certainly suited my case. I had lost my strength. I had become weary and faint. I needed to wait on the Lord. But what does "waiting on the Lord" mean in this twentieth century of radios and psychoanalysis? Is it just a sweet phrase to roll under your tongue like a Lifesaver, or is it something we workaday folks who don't understand Bible phrases can really do?

It is as practical as brushing your teeth. The divine power is all around us, above, below us, just waiting to pour into the stagnant pond of a sour, selfish life and transform it into a clear, sparkling stream. But sometimes the channels into our lives are clogged up. That's where our job comes in—to open up the channels. Maybe our bodies are out of tune. The greatest musician can't play on an untuned instrument. Maybe we have a habit that interferes. We need to look over all the avenues into our lives, check up on them, see that they are not dammed up. How long has it been since you made an inspection? No wonder some of our lives are foul and impure swamps, when our neglect has closed all the inlets. If you are a victim of these blue and insipid days, it is likely because the pipes into your room are out of order. You need to do a good job of plumbing before asking the Eternal to send the warmth of the Spirit and the Water of Life to your quarters.

Then, if you have fixed the connections, wait and the blessing will come. Maybe it won't come in a minute. Sometimes a drab spell is necessary to make the sunny days brighter. "All sunshine makes the desert." We enjoy things only by contrast anyway. If there were no darkness, eternal daylight would grow unbearable. It takes night to bring out the stars.

But the blessing will come to him who waits after he has opened the channels. After the plumbing comes the patience. And the "wait" of patience will remove the "weight" of our dull and tasteless hours.

November 20, 1927

79

Old Man Trouble

Some of us are lucky enough to get through this puzzle called *living* without going through a jail, hospital, or mental institution. But no mortal has ever succeeded in making the trip without meeting at all odd times and around unexpected corners that baffling character called Old Man Trouble.

He has been a puzzle from the start. The theologians and philosophers tried to explain him and invented ways to dodge or defeat him. But when we actually meet him, we forget, as usual, all the theories about him and proceed to handle him or be handled by him in some rather curious ways.

Some take the most abrupt way out by jumping into a river, or blowing out their brains, or turning on the gas, or by meeting eternity at the end of a hemp rope. Suicide never did appeal to me—it's too stylish nowadays. Whenever a thing becomes a fad, I'm off.

A second class of folks meets Old Man Trouble on his own ground. They get drunk. Instead of removing one trouble they add two more—a brown taste and a black conscience. There are some things you can do with Trouble, but it's a cinch you can't drown him.

Another crowd tackles him in a lighter vein. Their slogan is "What Difference Does It Make?" and they just laugh him off. That's a pretty good method sometimes. Most of our agonies become laughable later on. Did your sweetheart ever give you the air and have you pacing the floor at 2:00 A.M. with salty tears coursing down your pallid face while you sang bitterly "Someday, sweetheart, you may be sorry." A year or two later you tell your friends about it and laugh as you relate the horrible details. Why couldn't you have moved that laugh up a year or two and saved the agony? A laughing man is well prepared for Trouble but then some troubles are too deep for light treatment. Surgery is needed—not massage.

Some just "tough it out." Like Sir Walter Scott in his years of adversity, they adopt the stoic attitude, clinch their teeth, and endure it. They have no particular recipe for Trouble, except that they believe time will heal the wounds if they can manage to hold out. It is sometimes an admirable way when practiced by some people, but it is a cold and cheerless way and is adapted only to folks of strong and stalwart character.

Some meet the Old Man by the indirect method. They become absorbed in something else and let their particular trouble die for want of attention. They immerse themselves in some profession or cause or avocation and become so interested in a new affection that Old Man Trouble feels slighted and moves on. About the best way to get over losing your girl friend is to start out looking for another one. The indirect method is the best one so far.

A rare class of folks have found a more excellent way. Believing their way to be directed from above they accept Trouble, and if they cannot avoid or mollify it they say, "All is for the best." They believe that while all things are not good, all things do work for good to them who trust in a diviner direction than our own. There are countless arguments against this view and it has been pooh-poohed for centuries. But its adherents have been among the sweetest souls of earth and they have had amazing success handling Trouble.

The sophisticates and smart alecks laugh at that, but, strange to say, it works.

November 27, 1927

80

Priming the Pump

At this writing I'm in the northeastern corner of old North Carolina:

> Away down here in Pasquotank
> Where the bull-frogs jump from bank to bank.

It's a delightful section of God's earth, and it has held me all summer in its restful spell.

They use pumps down here instead of wells. Sometimes the pump is dry, and you have to pour water that you have saved in something else in order to prime it and get it going. Which teaches me a lesson.

We are like pumps. As the pump is planted in the ground, so are we all set down in the midst of life. Some of us produce great thoughts, great deeds, great dreams, great achievements. Some of us, like dry pumps, produce nothing. The fault is not with life but with us. There is water everywhere; the trouble is with the pump.

Perhaps we need priming. Sometimes we have to prime our lives from some other life to get it going. How many a man, useless, nonproductive, and a failure has been transformed into a blessing because some other life poured into his some of its inspiration and hope! Perhaps it was a friend, a sweetheart, or some great historic character. Anyway, his pump was primed and made productive.

Did you ever sit down to write or think and could not for love or money coax one idea from your lethargic brain? It is a good idea at such times to go about it indirectly. Read some good book or listen to some good music or go talk with a friend. In such a way you can sometimes borrow some water from another pump to start your own.

That is the value of good reading, good music, great pictures, or worthwhile conversation. They are not only valuable for their own intrinsic worth, but because they can be used to start a flood of thought in another life and awaken other minds to productiveness. Therefore, do not read and go to the movies or mix with people merely for transient satisfaction. Try to kindle your fires from other fires, prime your pump from the cisterns of other lives.

In living the Christian life, how often does the pump of the soul need priming? Business cares, frivolous concerns, indifference, and carelessness so easily run the pump dry. We feel no holy inspirations, the Bible seems dry, no worthy impulses challenge the soul. We try to become more spiritual, but there is only the hollow gasp and rattle of the dry pump. The soul needs priming.

If you have struck upon such spiritual dearth and dryness, perhaps it might help to get water from another pump. A good book, a sermon, an hour of worship, a chapter from the Bible, even a prayerbook may help to get you reconnected so you can pump for yourself. But they are only supplements—they cannot do your pumping for you. Some of us make that mistake. We swallow down sermons and books and advice galore, but we never do any pumping for ourselves. A Christian like that is about as useful as a pump that gives out only the water that you pour into it.

Some of us get mixed between our priming and our pumping. It is well to use the blessings of other minds and lives to spur our own to action, but we shall never know abundant and rich living until we go down underneath the soil of life and lay hold upon the Water of Life for ourselves.

And the Water of Life is always better when you get it for yourself than when you drink it secondhand from other lives.

September 11, 1927

189

81

Restoring Your Soul

Jesus, in describing to His disciples just what hard times lay ahead of them, added very significantly, "In your patience possess ye your souls."

It is as if He said: "You will fare hard in the days to come. You will be persecuted and hated and tried. But don't get excited amid your troubles. Keep calm and patient and move along coolly among your adversaries and you will possess your souls."

What does it mean to "possess our souls"? It means to retain our integrity, to sustain the unity and coherence of our inner life, to not go to pieces in the face of storm and stress.

We live in a feverish, tempestuous age when a thousand conflicting forces pull at our spirits and threaten to tear us into shreds. It is easy to lose our souls.

I do not mean here just what the professional evangelist means by losing our souls. This is in a different connection. Whenever we give way to evil influences and allow our integrity to be broken and breaches torn in our consistency and conduct, then we lose our souls. Then we need to have our souls restored. David knew this experience for he said, "He restoreth my soul."

But preventives are better than remedies, and it is better to so live that we do not lose our souls and need to have them restored. Happy is the man who moves calmly and serenely in the midst of life; whose heart is fixed on the eternal; and who does not break in the face of adversity nor leave the even tenor of his way every time bad weather or a toothache or a criticism or an unpleasant situation or a doubt comes along. Such a man possesses his soul.

I know a doctor whose smooth balance and restful serenity has always charmed me as it has others. He never grows fretful or excited or fidgety in the midst of the most upsetting conditions. When others are frantic and tense he moves about poised and even, talking in a soft voice, his very peacefulness helping to settle the raw and taut nerves of others. Such an attitude is not only indispensable to his profession but to his life—and to the lives of all of us.

Jesus was a perfect example of this spirit. Nothing upset Him. He was not in a hurry. He moved through all sorts of bedeviled situations and kept His soul. And, at last, when enemies were hounding Him and the cross loomed near He said to His excited followers, "My peace I give unto you."

In this neurotic, high-strung age, when so many lives run out in suicide, insanity, crime, and failure, we need seriously to set about possessing our souls. The only way out is to assume the Master's spirit and practice it daily until our own feverish self-life is displaced by His presence. It is not acquired in a day, but the most nervous and spoiled personality can become en-Christed by continual practice of the presence of God. Begin living like Jesus instead of yourself. It will be unreal at first, and you will forget and lapse into your old ways often at the beginning. But gradually His life will supplant yours until you can say, "Not I but Christ liveth in me."

Other things help. Avoid the modern rush as much as possible. Spend all the time outdoors you can. Nature is a great soother and restorer. Take time to be still and meditate. Look after your body for its weaknesses; things that harass the soul life. And keep "looking unto Jesus," not yourself.

So shall you retain the integrity of your character, keep your spirit intact, develop a coordinated personality, and "possess your soul."

May 26, 1929

82
Life's Little Loyalties

It is a dull, ordinary day. I am clerking in a little country store. Farmers are in the fields. Once in a while a car drifts by. All the birds are quiet in the shade. Across the hot sky a vagabond cloud floats now and then. It is a sultry, monotonous, commonplace day. Nothing exciting or interesting, no thrilling happening, no brilliant thought, no fine feelings, no noble inspiration. I am lazy, trifling, stupid, unambitious.

Such days we all know. No life can stay on a high key all the time. No one runs at full steam, top pressure, day in and day out. Into every life come the dull, drab seasons when nothing seems to kindle the pale embers of the spirit; nothing stirs the jaded soul. One reads and the same page that has enchanted us at other times is boresome. We try to think and the mind stalls. Perhaps we pray, and heaven seems locked. We can hardly endure ourselves. Others are tiresome and the whole world is hateful. We feel toward everything like the scoffer toward music when he sneered, "What are you crying about with your Wagner and your Brahms? It is only horsehair scraping on catgut!"

Yet we have no days more important than these. They test us as no others do. Anyone can be fine and splendid and noble once in a while when some special occasion stretches them to highest tension. The commonest soul may strain up to a fair showing in some big moment. It is the pale, tedious, insipid day that reveals our real soul stuff for what we are (when we are not trying) is what we *really* are.

It is said that no man is a hero to his valet. Few characters can carry through life's commonplace stretches without a breakdown somewhere. The temper will snap, the ideals will fade, cynicism and unpleasantness mar the spirit. Great is the man who can stand by the stuff and play the game when every bit of inspiration seems drained and nothing seems to matter. Most of us can measure up to a big chance once in a while, but not so many are true to life's little loyalties, when the world does not notice and we do not seem to care.

So instead of regarding such days as a loss, give them double attention. If you can master them, you never will face anything harder. If you can conquer the commonplace you need fear nothing. For they are the toughest stretches on this pilgrimage and more fade out along the ordinary grind than ever fall in the spectacular collapses.

Indeed, here is where the chain of character is forged; here we build most of the structure of our souls. For great spirits are not made in dazzling exploits and hair-raising performances; they are slowly and tediously grown by sturdy devotion to the best in the old grind of day by day, the school of life's little loyalties.

Sometimes I think Jesus spent thirty of His thirty-three years in the ordinary routine of Nazareth, conquering the commonplace. Nothing exciting happened there, but all the while the greatest achievement of history was being realized—Jesus was welding together the greatest character of all time. And He did it by steady devotion to the Eternal among life's little loyalties.

Your worst days may be your best days. And sometime what seemed your biggest moments may, in the perspective of time, become your poorest.

June 8, 1930

83

Faith and Trouble

Faith does not always change our circumstances but it does change us.

Many have entered the Christian experience expecting quick rewards in health, position, and possessions. They have been led to believe by certain detached Bible verses skillfully manipulated by immature enthusiasts that faith easily smashed all barriers, insured against trouble, and led invalids to abounding health and beggars to riches. They grabbed at faith as a sure-fire "Open Sesame" to visible rewards and earthly prosperity—and they have been disappointed. They still are poor, sick, or troubled, and very disillusioned.

Spiritual salvation does not mean temporal safety. It is no vaccination against trouble, nor does it immunize us against adversity. Sometimes we have more hardship after we set out to live the Christ life than before. Jesus promised His disciples persecution. Ananias was told in regard to the newly converted Paul, "I will shew him how great things he must suffer for my name's sake." God does not guarantee robust health, financial fortune, and earthly success to those who believe. It is well that He does not, else faith would become a cold business proposition and cease to be faith.

Faith does not promise ideal circumstances. It does master every outward condition and move mountains as Jesus said it would, but it changes them by changing us. It builds in us a spirit that no outward condition can bother, and when a man is victorious within, the without does not matter. Objective realities may be what they were before, but the man is different; his attitude has changed, and for him that changes everything. It is not things themselves but our way of looking at them that matters. Faith gives him the right perspective, and when he sees things as they really are they lose their terrors.

Fanny Crosby had a sublime faith, but she remained blind all her life. Spurgeon kept his gout, Sidney Lanier his tuberculosis. Paul was not saved from hardship. Adoniram Judson, the great missionary, lived in adversity until death. And Jesus' faith did not spare Him Gethsemane and Calvary. But their faith gave them sturdy souls that no outer circumstances could quench; carried them through their troubles to victory beyond. We know now that they were real successes here and are hereafter.

Many believers continue to have reverses. Sickness is theirs and grief and hardship. They lose their loved ones, banks close with their money, storms devastate their fields, and dark, dismal days threaten their faith. But if they are well grounded they will not whimper and whine. They will know that circumstance is purely incidental; that reality is not what we see but how we see it; that if we look at life from Christ's point of view no adversity can disturb us.

I pity the man whose faith can be swamped by one thunderstorm or one funeral. He still is a creature of circumstance, governed by earth's shifting moods. How much he needs the "victory that overcometh the world, even our faith."

February 15, 1931

84

Facing Trouble

We are continually hearing what life means to the rich, the successful, the prosperous. I wish some one would talk about what life means to the poor, the unsuccessful, the sick, and the unfortunate. Naturally, one would brag on life if it had been good to him. But a soul who can battle against lifelong adversity and still have faith—he is the man I like to hear.

At some time or other we must face trouble, disaster, misfortune. And then we do not want some shallow optimist with a Pollyanna grin, ladling out the stock platitudes so insipid that one is inclined to say what Job said to his comforters, "Is there any taste in the white of an egg?" For there is injustice and senseless misery in this world and oceans of bitterness that no smooth proverbs can mitigate and no logic solve. There are hateful situations and wretched circumstances that we can not make head nor tail of; the wicked prosper and the righteous suffer; fine lives snuff out early and devils live on and on; war and crime and poverty and pain drive men to wonder whether God is deaf or dead. One can not face such a world with a string of phrases nor unravel its evil with the yardstick of reason. Most of our comforters are pitifully inadequate.

While one may not presume to explain suffering and may honestly have to say again and again, "I can not understand," he is not thereby driven to the extreme of the pessimist and atheist. We can not explain anything for that matter; but we use a great many things and are the better for them. We are not primarily to figure out trouble nor even to bear it—we are to use it and, rightly used, some very fine things can be made of it. Incidentally, we may notice too that because we can see no reason for our trouble does not mean that no reason exists.

We do know that many souls, far from being driven desperate by adversity, have woven their mishaps into the makeup of splendid character. The one thing worth having in this world is character. One cannot have character without the possibility of evil, nor integrity without the opposing disintegrating forces, anymore than he can climb a mountain when there is no mountain to climb. In a world where there were no adverse conditions, one might have blissful innocence but not character. Trouble is therefore a challenge and one may surrender to it or master it through the spirit. One may not understand why adversity had to be, but one cannot very well have character without it, and character is always worth what it costs, no matter what it costs. No price is too great to pay for a coherent and unified soul.

The greater our trouble the greater in character we are if we master it. It may be a bitter struggle that drains us of every bit of moral energy at the time. But if we come out sturdier in our hearts, then we have converted it into a blessing and transmuted gall into glory.

There is the situation: hardship, sickness, failure, disaster, break upon us without reason and purpose so far as we can see. We can lambast the fates and renounce God and take the lower road of despair and death. Or we may meet our trouble as though there were moral purpose in it—whether we can see it or not—and overcome it in our souls though it kill the body. It is a tremendous alternative, and the witness of those fine spirits who took the upper road compared with the wretched example of the other kind ought not leave us long undecided which way to go.

November 24, 1929

197

85

Two Kinds of Peace

Not every one who has made peace with God has realized the peace of God.

Paul declares, "Being justified by faith, we have peace with God through our Lord Jesus Christ." Sin is a state of rebellion and discord, and man in his natural state is not in harmony with God. Men may admit the fact of God, write poems about Him, see Him in the creative sense in the world He has made, but human nature is out of tune with the Eternal. Of itself, it is not righteous and cannot be made so.

Of course this is not popular doctrine nowadays. Man has become very self-sufficient and seeks to educate and moralize himself into perfection. We are told that we should not call men sinners but rather appeal to the inherent good already in them and cultivate that. But Jesus declared, "That which is born of the flesh is flesh; and that which is born of the Spirit is spirit." There is an eternal distinction, and man is brought into harmony with God and makes peace with Him through Jesus only, who, being God and Man, made possible in His life and death our reconciliation. This has been made to sound as though God were peeved with the race and Jesus had to die to make Him friendly. Of course, it is exactly the other way around. We are alienated from God, and He so loved us that He sent Jesus to effect our at-one-ment. The depths of the atonement we never can fathom here, but it simply means that its provisions, when we accept them, set us at once at peace with God.

The atonement is treated lightly in some circles as a place of old-fashioned theology that cannot be reconciled with modern thought. That much is true: modern thought had better get reconciled with the atonement! When you take the atonement out of Christianity you have a bloodless and lifeless philosophy.

So we have peace with God. But many who have it do not move on to experience the peace of God "which passeth all understanding." The peace of God grows out of peace with

God; it is ours and waiting for us to claim it. We have entrusted our souls, our future, the issues of eternity, with Him and believe we shall be saved. But we ought to leave with Him as well all life's cares and burdens and worries and know the calm of His daily presence. If He can keep the larger issues, surely He can carry the smaller!

It is an age of noise and hubbub—feverish, restless, fretful, nerve-racking. The scarcest thing among us is peace. The world does not have it; and many of us believers allow care and fear and uncertainty to harass us quite as much as does the world. But no believer has any right to live so. Whoever was more battered by perverse circumstances than Jesus? Yet on His darkest day, He said to His followers, "These things I have spoken unto you. . . . Peace I leave with you, my peace I give unto you; not as the world giveth, give I unto you."

If you first have made peace with God, go on to realize His peace. Leave your concerns in His hand and believe He will hold them; simply trust and obey; if the old bothers come back to plague you, do not entertain them and shut the door in their faces. So shall the old attitude of worry and fear drop away and you shall grow into the tranquil sense of His presence. It is His will for you for "God hath called us to peace." And it is His promise for "Thou wilt keep him in perfect peace, whose mind is stayed on thee: because he trusteth in thee."

August 2, 1931

PART 10

Success, Sweet and Sour

86

There Is No Key to Success

In a day when so many platform pep-artists and professional ink slingers are preaching the gospel of "Getting There," it is well to remember that so far there is no certified key to the garden of success. Nobody has ever invented a trap that will snare that rare bird without fail every time it is set. There is no rule for success that works every time.

For success is a peculiar article. What is success for me might be failure to you and vice versa. A rule that would bring me the plums might bring you the sack. Each individual is entirely different and there is no uniform, stereotyped formula that will work out alike in every case.

Success is like courtship. There never has been an authorized rule for winning a girl's heart that will fit every girl. The tactics that would sound like wedding bells to one girl will sound like a dumbbell to another. Spouting poetry about springtime may work on Mary, but if you try it on Helen you may be giving yourself a free pass home. The only thing you can be sure of in courtship is that nothing is sure—you may get her and you may not, so you can only try and thus find out. Success is just like that.

And I'm glad it is. For what fun would it be playing Romeo if you were sure of the girl in advance—if you knew certain rules were bound to produce certain results? What would glory be worth if it were a dead certainty? It's the chance element in it that gives it charm and fascination and color.

Certain things enter into success. William Jennings Bryan was entirely right in attributing part of his success to pure luck, to events and circumstances and developments that he had nothing to do with. We may be, to some extent, the masters of our fate and the captains of our souls, but there are elements of luck (or whatever you choose to call it) quite beyond our control that play a big part in making us. Some men work as hard and display as many qualities of success as those who succeed and yet never arrive for reasons beyond their power to affect.

Willpower, determination, enthusiasm, ideals, persistence—a thousand and one things have been set down in the success books as steps up the tricky ladder to achievement. Some men have all the listed qualifications and never get anywhere. Some have only one or two and get there in a hurry. There are plenty of people as funny as Will Rogers, but he managed to find just the right spot on the public funny bone. Plenty of preachers are as good as Billy Sunday, but not many of us know it. The successful men are not necessarily superior to the rest of us because they got there—for some of them prove they are inferior *after* they get there. Call it shrewdness or luck or fate or superior judgment or understanding of human nature, there are weapons in the arsenal of the man who would storm the castle of greatness that will do the trick for one and not do it for another. It's a puzzling game, and there is no sure guidebook that will take you there for the simple reason that each man must blaze his own trail. There are plenty of men just as able as Cal Coolidge and Mussolini and Henry Ford and Lindbergh and Edison and Paderewski and Al Smith, who never reach the hilltop of success. Just why some do and some don't perhaps we shall never know.

And I'm thinking of that greatest success of all time, who died without the city gates the ignominious death of a criminal, on Calvary's brow. The greatest man since the dawn of time died, to all appearances, a failure. And it was He who said we must fail to succeed, must lose our lives to find them.

Success—a funny business, isn't it?

October 16, 1927

87

False Standards

Eric von Snoodle is just home from University, and he's the last word in Podunk. He's driving a new Goofus sport roadster; he wears a fraternity pin; he is the star halfback or drawback or something on the football team; and he can play a saxophone to beat thunder. Of course all the home girls are up in the air and the local Podunk sheiks are shining up their Fords and dragging out the best necktie for a hopeless competition. Eric is your typical, modern, American youth, and to tell the truth, all he is fit for is to be stuffed and mounted in a museum as an exhibit of the Nut Age Man.

David Lane lives in Podunk too, but he'll be no competition for Eric. Dave is considered a little old-fashioned and maybe a trifle off in the cerebellum. He camps down on the creek, reads poetry, goes to church, and had rather find a new bird than go to all the social blowouts in Podunk. He has a clean body, a fine mind, and a genuine character. But of course he has no Goofus roadster and his raiment is not what they wear at Bunk University, so pass him up and let Eric have his day.

But at the Great Assize "when earth's last picture is painted and the tubes are all twisted and dried," when the Master of all good workmen checks up on the job of life, real character will get the awards and the Erics will have about as much chance as a one-legged grasshopper in a Texas sandstorm.

Who is considered the leading chap in the young set of your town? It is a mark of tinny artificiality of this age that the boy who sets the pace in his burg is generally the bird with the most junk around him and nothing in him. It is the fellow with the cars and the clothes and the cash and the athletic record that is the paragon of modern youth. Listen to the average conversation about the ranking youngster of the locality and nothing is said about his integrity, his intellect, his spiritual appreciation. Those assets are obscured in a lot of chatter about his face, and his stylishness, and the speed of his car, and his baseball rating, and various other insignificant items.

It does not matter one whoop in Halifax whether or not you

can trace your family back to the time when some of your New England ancestors were hung on the lower limbs for horse stealing. It means but little whether you live on Millionaire Row or on a back street in Pruneville. What matters is character, and whenever anything but character is made the ideal of American youth, all our universities and fraternities and aristocracies, all the glitter and glare of this tinsel age will not save us from tumbling into hell.

The finest young man in America is the fellow who is clean in body, mind, and soul. He may drive a shot Ford, but he drives it with a sober head and a steady hand and doesn't try to stay on both sides of the road at once. He may wear ordinary duds, but he has brains enough to know that a bird is more than feathers, and that our greatest birds are plainest in plumage. He may not know all the latest jazz hits and dance steps, but he has found satisfaction in his head and heart instead of in his heels. When he passes by all the girls may not cry out, "There goes Eric—he's the hottest thing in town!" but all such prattle means no more to him than the chirping of the sparrows in the trees.

Look around over your hometown. Your real heroes may not all drive Goofus roadsters.

March 27, 1927

88

Hilda, the Girl that Ain't

Hilda lives down by a little, emerald lake in a tiny cottage almost smothered in old-fashioned roses. A modern landscape gardener might not call the design very elegant, but somehow that grassy slope rising from the water up to the house and then buried in a wilderness of flowers with little white gravel paths losing themselves all through it—that appeals to me more than all these modern yards with hot-house flowers, trying to look natural.

Hilda's parents didn't go in strong for antique crockery and transparent frockery, but they stocked their home with great books and good music. She was taught to love great literature and she found it more fascinating than modern novels and sex magazines. When other girls were munching candy and mooning over slushy romance and thrilling over silly movie heroes, Hilda was tramping the woods, camping by clear mountain streams, and learning the lore of bird and brook and blossom. When her feminine contemporaries were keeping unnatural hours and wasting energies on vapid emotionalism, she was swimming in the lake, canoeing in the river, her hair blowing in the wind, her face tanned, her body gloriously healthy.

Hilda is an interesting girl in this superficial age. She does not paint her face to apologize for having no color. She lets Mother Nature supply the cosmetics, and since Hilda has kept on good terms with her, Mother Nature has made a good job of it. It does me good to see one girl that can face the world with her mask off. I've seen so much paint in the last ten years that I'm color-blind, and looking at Hilda rests my eyes.

Don't get me wrong. She wears bobbed hair. She thinks the present style of clothes, sensibly worn, is better than her grandmothers'. She doesn't, however, parade as an advertisement that day by day in every way they're getting shorter and shorter. She does not know the "Charleston" and "Black Bottom," but she often dances alone in the woods and by the lake from the pure joy of living.

Of course Hilda knows that she is not keeping step with

progress. But it is doubtful whether she ever thinks much about how different she is. She grew up to naturally love such a life, and it rarely occurs to her that she is different. Certain it is she has lost no sleep because the Romeos from Bruneville never ask her for dates. And it isn't because they don't want them. Whenever Hilda goes to town (which is rarely), all of the local flappers take the second row. Pretty? Boy, when you see her coming you catch yourself asking, "Am I dreaming or am I ain't!" But those sheiks know that when they have a date with her, they have just a date with no trimmings, and most of them are after the trimmings, so they know it's no use to go. But she has the friendship and respect of every boy in town and the dirtiest-minded fellow there will wish in his best hours that all girls were as she. She is only eighteen, and many's the man who has already built in the sky of his hopes a dream castle with her as its princess.

Of course, the flappers are a little jealous, but I heard Julia Owensly talking about her the other night and she said: "That Hilda knocks my vocabulary cold. I can't place her. She's not like anybody else I ever saw. Not weird either, for she's as sweet as she can be, and I've never heard her say a shady word in my life. That time I pulled that raw joke over at her party—boy, the look she gave me made me think my heart had broke diplomatic relations. She gets a world more fun than I do with all my carousing. And she's the only person I ever heard who could talk about religion and make it sound as real as things that you really do. She's a problem to me: she's not old-fashioned and she's not weird, nor trying to pull any storybook stuff. I'd call it different, I guess, if that word hadn't been worn-out."

For fear I may be deluged with letters from idealistic swains, asking where said Hilda resides, let me say in closing, so far as I know, there ain't no such girl. I've been looking for her myself.

May 15, 1927

207

89
Cabins and Castles

I was riding with my friend through a little town. He was telling me who lived here and there.

We passed a massive, showy mansion that rose above his neighbors like a rich uncle among poor relations.

"There," said my friend, "is the home of our wealthiest citizen. He owns most of the town. A wicked old fellow. A regular crook, but he gets by with it."

I looked at the palatial home again and it seemed, as I looked, that the mansion faded away and in its place I beheld a squalid shanty, tumbled and almost in ruins. For a man who lives like that may seem to dwell in a castle but in truth he stays in a beggar's hut.

Later, quite out of town, we passed the humblest little cottage, worn and battered. But something about it, simple and calm and still, made me ask who lived there.

"Old Man Dunn," my friend informed me. "Poor in a way, owns a few acres, raises garden truck. But a good man—best man I know in these parts."

I looked at the cottage again and, as I looked, it seemed that the lowly cabin faded and in its stead rose a mansion fair, with airy spires as of some celestial city. For wherever a good man dwells, however it may seem to the passerby, there is a castle.

If we could travel up and down this land and see our dwelling places, not as they look but as they are, how many cabins would become castles, and how many mansions would give way to hovels! What a tremendous shaking up of society; what a rearrangement of our citizenry would result! How many of the upper crust would become plebians, and how many of the lowly would be lords! Verily, a new aristocracy would rise could we see things as they are.

We have ridiculous habits of appraising the homes we pass by the size of the house, the cost of the structure, the make of car under the carport. But could we lay aside these eyes of flesh and gaze through tawdry fixtures to spiritual realities,

Main Street might be a back alley and the "cream of the town" what we now rate curds!

For our real residence is not the pile of bricks or wood in which you eat and sleep. Your truest domicile is the structure you have built with the labor of your soul. Your actual dwelling place is that which you have constructed with the living timbers of things unseen. There is where you live.

And if you have built only with wood and stone and mortar and starved your soul, you may have the showiest house in town, but in truth you are a poor, starved beggar in a ramshackle hut. And if you are a good man you may dwell in some log cabin, as houses go, but in your heart you live in a castle divine.

Where do you live? Cabin or castle? Do you dwell on Main Street in the kingdom of God?

"In my Father's house are many mansions," the old version reads. I am thinking that only those who have built for themselves castles of the soul while here below can be ready to move into the upper mansions. And many a mansion dweller here in the world of sight will find that his furniture does not fit in the palaces of God.

December 9, 1928

90

Personality or Character?

The world has gone wild over personality, that elusive something we have tried to define in all sorts of terms from the "It" of Clara Bow pictures to the metaphysical abstractions of magazine schools of psychology. Everybody is studying how to be one of those knockout human dynamos that walk into a room and literally electrify the very air with personal magnetism—or that is what we read one can do though I never have seen it done.

Libraries are full of it, platforms proclaim it, magazines are crammed with ads from all sorts of fantastic cults with weird names and more weird claims. They promise to take your bashful farmhand from his plodding existence behind the plow and, after a few lessons by correspondence, so transform him by his latent powers, inner self, subconscious mind, or some such indefinite part of his innards that within a few weeks he is liable to elope with the landlady.

Whatever personality is, we all want it. But there is something far better—and that is character. "He that ruleth his spirit [is greater] than he that taketh a city." Personality is partly a gift, and while it is often charming and attractive and scintillates in the drawing room, it may grace a sinner as well as a saint—a devil as well as a divine. It is a dangerous thing where there is no conscience and principle to guide it, and its winning ways have snared countless souls into hell.

We had better seek character, well-knit moral integrity. It may not be so thrilling to those superficial surface skimmers who live on life's foam, but it will endure when mere smartness and attractiveness have struck the wall. It may not be recognized by these social puppets who are out for life's glitter and not its real gold, but it does not care how the world receives it, whether with bricks or bouquets.

When storm and strife break upon us, a charming personality is not enough. Plenty of lovable, interesting souls are collapsing in suicide, sickness, and sin before the ravages of adversity. Then, only sturdy and rugged character built steadily through years of fine loyalty, can carry through.

A winning personality is good, so far as it goes. But as with many other things nowadays, we are carrying it further than it goes. I have known some fascinating types who were not worth killing. And I have known some rugged mortals, rough but genuine, to whom I know I could go and find dependable friendship when the butterflies had flitted away.

Of course, "contrive to mix 'em." But if you are not the highly charged human battery upon whom all eyes focus when your dynamic presence irradiates the room, lose no sleep. The world's great work is done by wallflowers. The popular and famous in the center of the show get nothing done but acknowledge compliments. The obscure, not being bothered, have time to work. And one day the fawning gushers grow tired of their idols, and turning, behold that life's real master-pieces are done by those toilers in the night who did their deeds and scorned to blot it with a name.

A fool may have personality. No fool can have character. Do something a fool can't do.

November 2, 1930

91

Greater than Lindbergh

Just when everybody is whoopin' 'er up for Brother Lindbergh, it may be undiplomatic, to say the least, to break the harmony with a different tune. But I am noted for saying the right thing at the wrong time, and since I have no great reputation to lose, here goes.

Lindbergh has pulled a great stunt. Far be it from me to pluck one twig from the laurels that crown his courageous brow. Any man who can sit in a one-engined air-buggy with the Atlantic Ocean under him and the Milky Way above him and yet keep saying, "Sail on and on!" until he gets where he started is a modern Columbus and deserves all the buttons and jewelry that he can lug. I don't begrudge the honors he got over there. I'm willing to give Lindbergh a hooray along with the rest. But something else keeps bobbing up in my mind.

The greatest heroes of earth do not get into the papers nor are they offered fabulous sums to enter the movies. There is nothing very dramatic and theatrical about them, and to exhibit them wouldn't mean much mazuma at the ticket office. Mothers who wear themselves out in the weary routine of the home, yet glorify life's commonest tasks with the radiance of love—these are our heroes. Dads, who plug along in old-fashioned clothes with suspenders, skimping that their sheiks and flappers may have it better; sick folks who lie flat on their backs through tiresome years, yet manage to stay sweet; teachers who stay in the background that others may come to the front; missionaries on the frontiers of civilization, dying in obscurity that men may live in the Light; plain folks who fail in business and see their fairest dream castles tumble into ruins, yet are not sour and spoiled—these are the great of earth. Nobody decorates them for they do nothing sensational; nobody writes them up, for their achievements make poor reading for a thrill-crazy world.

The performance of Lindbergh required only a few hours. The poorest of us can hold up long enough to do something remarkable maybe once in our lives. But the man who can hold to an ideal year in and out, who can sustain his enthusiasm when no expectant crowd looks on and no one knows how hard is his struggle, that man is a hero of the finest class, for such work calls not merely for nerve and daring but for *character.* Plenty of people can be great for a little while, but not many of us can be great within all the time when no one notices nor honors us for it.

To be sure, Lindbergh had to study and prepare for years to be able to do what he did. But it is not that phase of it that comes in for attention. It is the sudden performance, cut off from all his preliminary training, that is magnified. It tends to exalt the short spurt of heroism above the long grind of patient continuance in great living.

The plodding worker of the old school gets scant encouragement when some upstart with less preparation and ability by some twist of fortune rises over his head to a place far ahead of him. But for all the appearances, the great man is he who has mastered his work through long hours of faithful application, whether the press and the movies ever know it or not.

June 12, 1927

213

92
Which Way Prosperity?

It is very significant that, during the last presidential campaign, the paramount issue was the return of prosperity. Moral issues were cast aside, and one heard next to nothing of the need of ideals and spiritual guidance. The foundations of this land were laid in faith in God, and character was a prime asset. 1932 found us interested only in whatever promised to fill the Ford with gas once more and place a chicken in every pot.

Talk nowadays of the need of moral leadership and vision, and the audience sleeps. Picture a return to the drunken spree of materialism that preceded 1929, and everybody sits upright. No matter what it takes to bring back prosperity, let us have it. If liquor will bring it(!), give us liquor. If demagoguery or dictatorship will do it, give us a Mussolini. The American people see no higher now than a life that consisteth in the abundance of things a man possesseth.

The nation is sold out to tomorrow. Everything the average man has was bought on that most delusive and insane principle of "Get it now and pay for it sometime." A nation crowded with schools and colleges had no more sense than to think it could cheat the old principle of "Pay as you go." Railroads today owe bonds that will mature after trains are as obsolete as the family carry-all. From that on down the scale to the small fry who live on the credit of every business in town, the whole country has dared to violate the eternal principle of "Owe no man any thing, but to love one another." Now we owe everything and don't love one another.

There is a prosperity in keeping with the Word of God but not many want that sort. Says Joshua 1:8: "This book of the law shall not depart out of thy mouth; but thou shalt meditate therein day and night, that thou mayest observe to do according to all that is written therein; for then thou shalt make thy way prosperous, and then thou shalt have good success." Here is the law of true prosperity: to keep the Word of God, to read it, and to heed it.

Psalm 1:3 says of the righteous man, "whatsoever he doeth

shall prosper." He may not always get rich; he may be poor and suffer much adversity, but if his life is in the will of God all things work together for good to him, and he is a spiritual success regardless of outward appearances. But the world does not care for that kind of prosperity. It seeks the kind that keeps up with the Joneses, that puts itself forever in debt to maintain the pitiful paraphernalia of care and clothes and houses and furnishings—the trivial trappings of modernity's mad masquerade.

We Americans have never learned what true prosperity is, and we are in no spirit to attain it now. We thought we were rich and increased with goods and had need of nothing and knew not that we were wretched and miserable and poor and blind and naked. May we yet buy gold tried in the fire and white raiment that we may be clothed, and anoint our eyes with eye salve that we may see.

January 29, 1933

93

Good—For Pay

The success magazines feature the cut-and-dried "How I Got This Way" article by some notable who has attained to the presidency of a bank or the season's best-seller. The public devours these little autobiographies with all the gullibility for which it is noted, particularly the inevitable set of rules for making dreams come true—forgetting that each man must write his own code. They gulp them down, not so much because they are good, but because the writer is head of the Whoozit Concern or author of the latest hit.

I would like to read an article by some man who has played the game but missed the headlines—some failure who recommends the upright path for some other reason than because it led him to a fortune or fame. I'm rather tired of the stereotyped lectures of the high and mighty who managed to cash in on their goodness for the directorship of a railroad or the chief seat in a synagogue. Of course they will advocate the stock virtues of the moralizer. Who wouldn't boost the thing that made him rich! I will listen better to the man who is good—but not because it paid!

There are splendid and noble souls scattered up and down this land who are the salt of the earth and moral cement that holds it together—but they will never get into the success periodicals, for their goodness did not seem to pay. There is nothing illustrious and spectacular about them. They never chanced upon that stroke of luck that pitches a few into the limelight. They had no hair-raising adventures that the public craves, nor were they peculiarly smart. Still, they stay good and one wonders why.

Their lives are not the Pollyanna sort composed of one long grin. They live in peevish families and wait on grumpy patients and raise provoking babies and work for hateful bosses and hold the sack while some one else gets the plums. They try to sing and their voices crack, they write for the wastebasket, they invest in stock that always drops, they look for ships that never come in. The rules that put the other fellow in a president's chair put them in a wheelchair. Yet they stay good, though it does not pay.

Nor am I coming around to the hackneyed wheeze that "although it didn't pay in dollars and cents it paid in inner satisfaction, and so forth." They do not dwell in happy bliss, singing all day long. Doubts bother them, fevers harass them, the perplexing turns of life often puzzle and make them sad. But they plan on in spite of it and stay good and actually become better.

It is a precious thing wherever you find it, this goodness that goes unrepaid. These are the heroes without the halos, the souls that sing while they stifle sobs and look upward through tearful eyes. Often wondering why things go as they do, they do not give up the dream because they can not make it come true.

These are the real successes. They do not sit in easy chairs and preach "Do as I did because you see what I got for my goodness." They are good in spite of what they got—good because the pursuit of goodness is sweeter than the possession of everything else.

I would like to read an article by one of these. But our modern public measures everything by what it pays and the man who can show no dividends is rated "broke." So we shall continue to hear from the good boys who cashed in.

May 5, 1929

94

A Word to the Go-Getters

This is for the modern go-getters, so glorified nowadays—the typical successful Americans who are buying and selling and storing up goods and gold; whose eyes are set on the things of earth (its mansions and estates and styles and luxuries); whose only language is shop; whose church is the marketplace; whose god is the dollar.

Stop a minute in your wild chase, wherever you are—at home, in the hotel, the office, the Pullman, or out on the road with your briefcase trying to convince some apathetic prospect that yours is the best yet.

Do you realize that you and the junk man with his rags, bottles, and old iron are following the same business? Here you go, burning out your bearings, raking and scraping together—*what?* Simply junk, the only difference being that yours is new junk, while the trashman's junk has the advantage of seniority. Go out to the edge of town and look at the dump heaps and say to yourself, "Here is what the go-getters of a few years ago accumulated." The junk pile is the go-getters monument.

Are you trying to gain the world? Beware, lest you awake some coming day in the midst of your prosperity to learn that while you were tearing down old barns to build greater, the best in life slipped by. It is so easy to lose the best chasing the good.

Nothing is more tragic than the rich man who has spent a life working himself up to where he might live at leisure, only to find that somewhere in the mad melee he has lost the appreciation for the finer things that he now has time to enjoy.

When the Bible says: "What shall it profit a man if he shall gain the whole world and lose his own soul?" it does not mean by "soul" some mystic part of us to be saved for use in the next world. It means that divine faculty within us that appreciates and enjoys all the finer spiritualities of life. It is hard for the go-getter to keep his soul.

Somehow the great souls of earth do not wait for safe finan-

cial investments to set them free. It is given to few men to follow the stock market with their left eye and the things of the
spirit with their right. They become wall-eyed or blind in the
right. The Master was indulging in no metaphorical exaggera-
tion when he spoke of the camel and the needle's eye.

Is it not strange that so many businessmen who pride themselves upon practical common sense are not using common
sense at all? Is it not nonsense to gain the world and pay for it
with your soul? Is not the poor man who carries little earthly
baggage but is rich in the spirit—is he not the true businessman after all? Isn't he using the best common sense of the
two?

We talk of businessmen, meaning only those who traffic in
the tangibles of earth. But there are two sorts of business: the
business of earth and the business of the spirit. The man who
follows either is a businessman. If the business of the spirit
pays better and bigger dividends than the business of
earth—which it does, beyond all computation—then, who is
the best businessman?

The question is not Are you a go-getter? but What do you
"get" when you "go"?

July 27, 1930

95
Spring Notes

It is early spring and the advance notices have arrived. There is green among the trees and red along the waterways. The call of the flicker and the sound of the dove are heard in the land. On my morning stroll I stopped on the bridge to hear the yellowthroat and white-eyed vireo among the reeds. From the moss-hung cypress swamp came the clear, wild challenge of the water thrush.

Down the road I fared, teasing on the way Solomon, the black handyman in the community; he goes to sleep when he sits down to think over his troubles. Then I went on by a roadside shack where old Aunt Nancy was singing a hymn with high notes beyond the range of any songbook. I chatted awhile on the edge of a field with a young plowman who had been impressed by my Sunday-night sermon. On my way back I saw three cardinals.

I am so glad to be a country preacher. It is good to live in a place like Weeksville, which cannot be found on the map. It is more fun to be from Weeksville than from Washington, for instance. Recently I spoke in Philadelphia, and everybody wanted to know just where my village could be found. Now I would not have had the pleasure of telling them if I had been from Washington, for everybody knows where Washington is!

You might laugh at my salary, but there are other compensations. Of course, a country preacher does not rate so highly in some church conclaves, nor is he often greeted in the market-places as *Rabbi*. But one can forego that for the freedom of woods and fields and the privilege of living simply and plainly. And we think of One who grew up in humdrum Nazareth, who loved little Bethany, who preached outdoors.

Our complex civilization has almost driven solitude and meditation out of our lives. Said Statesman Newton D. Baker: "The effect of modern inventions has been to immeasurably increase the difficulty of deliberation and contemplation about large and important matters. I doubt whether there could have been a Constitution of the United States if the deliberations of the Constitutional Convention had been currently reported by radio, telegraph, and timely newspapers over the whole extent of the thirteen Colonies." I wonder whether Bryan could have made his "Cross of Gold" speech half so well through a microphone. When the radio came, oratory languished, for who can be microphone-conscious and message-conscious at the same time?

The hurry and bustle of this practical and impersonal age has almost eliminated the human-interest element from professions. There was a deep wisdom about the old country doctor (who knew all his patients by their first names) that the most efficient specialist sorely needs to add spirit to the letter of his lore. The up-to-date minister is threatened with losing the personal touch beneath an avalanche of clubs and committees. All of us need to beware lest being careful and troubled about many things we forget the one thing needful.

From my window I can see the redhead at work in the tree nearby; the myrtle warblers leisurely play along; here and yonder are the welcome pink and white of peach and plum, early banners in the march of spring; everywhere are farmers busy in the level fields with the old, old wonder of seed and soil. One cannot help reflecting that if this present earth can be so lovely how wondrous will His redeemed creation be!

April 16, 1933

96
What Is Your Life?

Paul said, "For to me to live is Christ."

For you to live is—what?

With some it is money. But "a man's life consisteth not in the abundance of things which he possesseth." So that is the wrong estimate of life. Money is worth something but it is not worth living for. We are only tenants in this world; nothing is ours anyway and "to have is to owe, not own." So why bother collecting what is not ours?

For others to live is appearances. They are not so anxious to be rich as to be thought rich. They put everything in the show-case and keep nothing on the shelves. Life is a masquerade with them, and they are hard put to it to keep up the pose. They are not characters but clowns feverishly racing to keep up with the Joneses. In fact, it is this estimate of life that keeps the noses of most of us to the grindstone. For it is not the high cost of living but of keeping up appearances that taxes us. Those who live for looks also are wrong for "man looketh on the outward appearance, but the LORD looketh on the heart."

For some to live is success, popularity, fame. I once longed to be famous, but after looking around at some who already were I was cured. "All success is but a prison and only those who fail are free." Anyone with a good press agent can be famous nowadays. Courting popularity is a tricky affair—one day you get bouquets, the next day bricks. It is a poor estimate of life for, as John says, "the pride of life . . . passeth away . . . but he who doeth the will of God abideth forever."

For many, to live is pleasure. But those who live for pleasure do not find it for it is not a business but a by-product. We gather it only as we give it. The Bible puts it, "She that liveth in pleasure is dead while she liveth," so that certainly is not life's proper estimate.

Paul said, "For to me to live is Christ." Now to some of us Paul's career may look rather uninviting. An outcast Christian Jew, persecuted over the face of the earth, sickly and often discouraged, being jailed and whipped and stoned and shipwrecked, sewing tents for a living, a despised preacher of an unpopular religion—not many comfortable moderns would care for that. But Paul had what moderns do not have: he had found *life*, its true ideal and estimate. And because he had, he had reached that happy point where no matter what happened to him he was satisfied. To live was Christ, to die was gain. Either way he looked, the prospect was pleasant. We are always worried over what may happen to us, and we are forever building barriers against hardship and adversity. But Paul did not care. He had learned to abound and to be in want. Everywhere he looked he saw Jesus. True, he saw also trouble and pain but they were only incidental. With us they are the main thing, for we never have reached that point where the temporal is swallowed up in the eternal.

G. Campbell Morgan has pointed out that one must have Paul's estimate of life to have his estimate of death. Only those who can say, "For to me to live is Christ," can also say, "To die is gain." You cannot say, "To die is gain," after saying, "To live is money, appearances, success, pleasure." We are afraid of death, and only those who have found Christ have lost that dread, for only Christ has conquered the grave.

For you to live is—what? If Christ is your estimate of life, then you have found the true and proper valuation of everything in life, of death, and all that lies beyond it.

August 19, 1934

223

PART 11

On the Road

97

The Other Side of the Hill

Nothing is so fascinating to the hiker, swinging along circuitous mountain roads, as the lure of the other side of the hill.

Several years ago, with knapsack and walking stick, I tramped for days through crooked Blue Ridge trails. And always just a few yards ahead lay another curve with all the mystery of its other side. What vistas waited for me around that bend? What panorama would the next turn reveal? The whole journey was kept atingle with the romance of the other side of the hill.

It is so in life. Anticipation is the spirit of the other side of the hill. What we have and know already often turns out dull and tasteless. When the pursued becomes the possessed, it takes on another—for the loss of glamour. But life is never all past and present. There is still another curve, and who knows what beyond it? So our weary souls keep plodding, maybe a bit disillusioned with what was and is, but still hope challenges us to what shall be—the other side of the hill.

We could not long endure were life one long, straight track without its mystic curves. Business crashes, health fails, friends depart, cherished dreams collapse—yet somehow with occasional exceptions where poor sports take poison to end the game, most of us carry on. It is the other side of the hill that does it. Maybe next year will be better. Maybe we shall get well in spite of the doctor's verdict. Perhaps we shall find better friends than we lost. Possibly the next castle will not tumble. We still have faith in the other side of the hill.

Indeed, that is what faith is: confidence in the other side of the hill. We know so little of life, of truth, of God and destiny. Most of them lie beyond our ken around the curve of knowledge. But from what we have seen we judge there must be more, so we trust and travel always questing for what lies around the other side of the hill.

Is not this the supreme charm in people themselves? The most interesting person does not put all his wares on the counter. He gives you the impression of vast hidden reserves, of a storehouse of personal treasure of which what you see is but a sample. We cultivate the fellowship of friends, sweethearts, or loved ones because we want to know more about them. What we know is an everlasting enticement toward the unknown. Happy is the friend, the sweetheart, the wife, the husband who stays a little mysterious, who does not become common in familiarity—who partially stays in a very sweet way around the other side of the hill. The coquette "keeps 'em guessing." In a finer sense than the coquette uses it is a good policy. Do not live entirely on this side of the hill.

Finally we shall approach the last hill, the ultimate curve. We call it *death* and drape it in black and in its presence play mournful dirges. But why? How do we know that it is bleak and desolate? From this side it may look forbidding enough but it too has another side. And I am thinking that for him who meets it well, there await around the bend finer vistas and landscapes more sublime than ever we have known. So we shall tilt the hat and throw back the shoulders, swing our stick, and hum a song, for through the Valley of the Shadow of Death He leadeth us to worlds far finer than this—just around the other side of the hill.

December 8, 1929

98

Pilgrims and Strangers

Yesterday as I set out on my usual stroll, I was approached by an elderly gentleman who is visiting near me. He is a man of some means, a widower who spends part of his time among his children, and who has traveled extensively. He is splendid company, and I was glad to have him walk a way with me. But he started off on a vein that set me thinking.

"I think I'll get a walking stick like yours," he began, "and take up walking. I've got the blues this evening—nervous temperament anyway. Do you know, I read one of your pieces where you said we seek happiness in travel and always come back home more homesick than ever. That is certainly true, for I stay here a while and there a while, but pretty soon I must up and away, for I'm never satisfied."

I was struck with what he said, for I am his type—of a nervous makeup—always questing for something that must surely lie just around the next corner. I, too, have rambled most of my time and have often felt the sweet futility of vagabondage.

After all, we are only a race of pilgrims and strangers in an unknown universe. After thousands of years of speculation and study and philosophy we know but little as to whence we came or where we go. Occasionally some smart aleck thinks he has worked out all the details of his origin and destiny, but most of us (if we are honest) will admit that the whole works is a rather puzzling affair. We are a bunch of vagabonds in a strange country.

We gather to ourselves much possessions only to discover that we cannot enjoy them. We make money and learn that only the trivial things of earth are bought and sold. We travel and ever with us goes that unutterable loneliness, that nostalgia of the soul so independent of time or place. We are famous and find no joy in it; we are unknown and wear ourselves out trying to be famous. We dabble in learning and find it a weariness; we go in for pleasure and find it to be pain. And on we wander, chasing rainbows, dreaming dreams, seeing visions, forever questing until "dust to dust and ashes to ashes" relegates another tramp to his final parking place. There is something wistful, pathetic, tragic about it all, this ramble called *living,* these hobos called *men.*

But it is exactly that which makes life adventurous and interesting. Who would want to make this trip if every step of it were certain and marked out in advance? The most miserable poor wretch in this world is the peg-in-a-hole who is perfectly content. Give me the lure of the uncertain trail; don't let me die of the ennui and boredom of knowing exactly where I am!

So far from being a damper to hope and exuberant living, to know that I'm a pilgrim and stranger is a challenge to my faith. I don't understand the why and wherefore of existence, I do not know just why I'm here nor what lies beyond the cradle and the grave. I simply have to make a big guess at it one way or another and live out my guess. So I dare to believe that it all means intensely and means well: that we came from somewhere and are headed somewhere; that there is *purpose* and *mind* and *meaning* behind and in and through it all. And even if I am wrong I will be the better off, for I had rather live as though there were meaning in it and be wrong than to creep through life in unbelief and despair and be right. In fact, I can't be wrong, for the very fact that my way works best proves its rightness.

August 7, 1927

99

Life's Detours

We were pleasantly rolling along on the smooth highway when around a curve we met that loathsome DETOUR sign. Turning abruptly, it went into a rough, unpromising, little dirt road that strayed off down a dismal hill. There were loud grumblings and growlings of the tourist sort, and a lambasting of the authorities who forever built roads and never had any open all the way to anywhere.

So off we put. And found that our drab little trail led through lovely meadows and blossoming orchards and healthful uplands by quaint homes and old mills and rustic retreats we never would have seen along the highway. It was a glorious relief from rushing traffic, patent-medicine signs, and gas stations, and we were sorry when the detour ended.

Is it not so with life? We set out upon the highway of some fixed course we have chosen and mapped and planned for ourselves. Then one day, around some sudden bend of the road, we find our thoroughfare blocked and the side road in its place. Business crashes, health fails, dear ones die, disaster comes; we must abandon the way we meant to go and try some shabby trail of shattered dreams and fallen hopes and breaking hearts. We start out wearily upon it and find to our surprise that it leads to treasure and beauty we never would have found elsewhere.

The finest scenery of life is often along its detours. The smoother boulevards seem more pleasant, but we ride so easily we fall asleep. Or if we stay awake we talk too much or fret over the baggage or miss the landscape, straining to reach our destination. We can not speed along the detours, so there is time to stop to look around and see.

A boy writes me that his father's death means giving up college to help care for smaller brothers and sisters. He is all broken up about it. He has struck a detour. He will perhaps find along that side road, if he travels it nobly, a better education than textbook and preceptor can give him. He need not be blue. The side road has its compensations.

Everywhere we find these pilgrims of life's detours. Invalids and cripples who gave up rosy dreams for drab infirmity; despondent souls whose best and dearest friends have passed; humble laborers who planned greater deeds than circumstance allowed them to do; travelers who set out running and now plod along with a crutch. A great host there are but they are the salt of the earth. They are happier than the limousine idlers on the boulevards. They are more wholesome and tolerant and sweet. Life's detours have shown them greater things. Their strength is made perfect in weakness. One hears of the survival of the fittest. Those apparently most unfit are perhaps our fittest. The side road breaks a man but makes him over and better for the break.

Bunyan detoured by Bedford Jail—and found *Pilgrim's Progress*.

Paul detoured on the Damascus Road—and is immortal.

Jesus detoured by Golgotha—to save a world.

May 19, 1929

100

Breezing Along with the Breeze

Vagabondage is the best antidote for provincialism.

After all, the tramp represents something in life that we modern folk are losing at our peril.

If there is anything that we have gone in for with all our might today, it is one standardized way of living. The ideal citizen is the efficient, businesslike, practical chap with a salary, an office, a good car, a home, and a small family. He is a regular, orderly, conventional person, and the fellow who dares to break these established precedents is utterly lost to a methodical world.

We have become so businesslike that we need a good supply of tramps to save us from stagnation. We have become so tied to offices and positions and money making that we are dying of dry rot. And a few hours of golf or an evening at a ball game do not supply our lack. We are born gypsies and wanderers, and the spirit of the vagabond is in us. We must keep it alive lest we lose the romance and color and adventure of living in the sea of commercialism. The thousands of automobile tourists who travel over our country the year round are an encouraging sign that humanity will not be kept caged. It must have blue sky and breezes, the thrill of wide horizons, and the joy of the open road.

If you have been sticking to a sedentary job till you feel as inanimate as your typewriter; if your joints are rusty, your blood runs lazily, and your nerves are on edge—take up respectable hoboing if you possibly can. Get out of that stuffy office, lock the door behind you, and draw out some of that money you've earned with a resolution to waste it on the best investment you ever made. Get yourself a khaki suit, walking shoes, a slouch hat, a knapsack, and a good, stout stick. Then take to the road and see where it takes you. Let the wind blow through your hair, let your face grow brown and leathery, drink from wayside wells and springs, and sleep wherever you can. If folks look at you a little suspiciously from the corners of their eyes, remember they're just dying to be like you but their respectability won't let them do it. Learn the magic lore of the road, let the spell of the gypsy trail make you drunk with its witchery. Feast yourself on the delights of the road to anywhere, the blue sky, green fields and running brooks, bird songs and blossoms, the wistful charm of dawn and sunset. You will feel more keenly your kinship with all the universe, and God will become intensely real. The poor, artificial person that you were back in the office will gradually slough off, and you will come out of your businesslike shell the being that you originally were and that you really are—a waif in a wide and unknown universe, a tramp on this little bit of a star swung between two eternities.

I like that song "Breezing Along with the Breeze." I think it is a happy expression of the gypsy soul that is in us all and often so pitifully smothered in the dust of a workaday world. And I think we owe something to the Tattered Tommies and Weary Willies whose insatiable itch for the open road will not let them settle down and fit into our scheme of things. I never see a tramp but he suggests to me something whimsical and untrammeled and free—an atmosphere that, for all his crudities, is appealing to those caught between the millstones of progress. They are a relief to us who are so tired of seeing things done decently and in order and in keeping with the latest on business efficiency.

Take to the vagabond trail if you can. And if the legalists are shocked and the circumspect deplore your taste, remember that the greatest of men was a vagabond and had no where to lay His head.

May 22, 1927

101

Florida Musings

One winter I went a-camping to Florida in a Ford with the customary tent, frying pan, and other accessories strapped on all sides. That really is the only first-class way to travel. Pity the poor souls who are forced by circumstances to stay in the palatial hotels! It is one of life's odd turns that the happiest travelers most often go third-class. Look not for light hearts in the limousines on Main Street; there will be more joy amongst a group of laughing young people on some shady side street.

What a strange creature is man! He wears out his days gathering what he thinks to be the price of pleasure. Then, one day he builds his "retreat" by some favored spot exactly as the travel folders picture it. He comes out in his light clothes and two-tone oxfords, the basking vacationist, exactly as specified. And then he wakes to the fact that, somewhere along the road, he lost the power to enjoy and appreciate what his money can buy—in gaining the world he has lost his soul. His crusted heart, as metallic as the dollars he has hoarded, has about as much romance as his adding machine. And far lighter in spirit is the moneyless caddy who carries his golf clubs!

I stood on Miami corners and watched the well-to-do ride by. No one noticed me, a vagabond preacher with a few dollars in his pocket and a blanket on the ground for his bed. *And yet,* thought I, *some of you who float so breezily by would gladly exchange for my treasure!* For I have found life and God and the gateway to peace that money cannot open.

We call ourselves wise but is it wisdom that creates fairylands of loveliness and then sits down with empty, hungry hearts, unable to enjoy them? Coral and stucco, seashell walks and dreamy patios, sunny skies and blue water, cannot rest the soul of man.

Long ago, there dwelt among us One who had no home, no pillow for His head. But He had rest and so has every soul "that leans on Him for repose." For rest belongs not to any place but to the Person.

One evening, while I lived in the languid lowland near the

Carolina coast, I strolled along beset with doubts and questionings. A little way before me down the sleepy road an old woman ambled along. She hummed as she walked, and soon the hum burst into song as only country folk can sing:

> In the cross of Christ I glory
> Towering o'er the wrecks o' time.

There was the secret of serenity and peace that mansions and money cannot bestow! Thanks be to God for unsearchable riches open to all who will trust and obey; so marvelous that it transcends all mortal wisdom as the sun transcends the candle; yet so simple that, if she will, an old black woman may invest therein and find joy that breaks into such a song as my weary heart drank in that evening down in "the flat country," along a lazy road in the glow of a summer sundown.

September 20, 1936

102

By Saginaw Bay

This preacher is on the conference grounds by beautiful Saginaw Bay in Michigan, preaching and listening to other fellows preach during these August days. A splendid group of preachers, mostly Baptists, who stand for the truth in these days of apostasy, and a fine crowd of Michigan folk make up a most responsive audience.

Last night we gathered in the yard and sang gospel songs and choruses until late. There is a blessed growing revival spirit over our land. Sometimes we get under the juniper tree like Elijah and conclude that all the good folk are gone with the exception of ourselves. The favorite shade tree of many Christians is the juniper. If more of us were under Nathanael's fig tree in prayer, we should have less time or inclination to visit the juniper.

There are more good people over the land believing the Word and living for Christ than we sometimes imagine. And God is raising a growing testimony among His people of all denominations and a fellowship of prayer and praise looking for the Lord's return but meanwhile praying for a real awakening.

Some of the major denominations are putting special emphasis on evangelism. This is good if it is not merely a worked-up phase of denominational work, undertaken and engineered in the strength of the flesh. And let it not be forgotten that revival must precede evangelism. The need of real revival in our churches has been passed over very delicately, and the emphasis put upon winning the lost. But the result too often is that we gather in new swarms of converts into our churches too often with a profession but without a real possession. It is significant that in the New Testament not so much is said about going out after the unsaved. The main emphasis is placed on feeding and stirring up the saints, for if they get on the job in the power of the Spirit, they will naturally go after the lost. When the lost joy of salvation is restored and we are upheld by God's Spirit, then transgressors shall be taught His ways and sinners converted unto Him.

God is raising up many other agencies outside the regular denominational forces. Laymen's groups are springing up all over the land. Often the regular churches fail, and God raises up the irregular and unusual. He has done it all the way down through the ages. Wesley and Whitefield were God's instruments in their day to call a nation back to God when the churches had gone to sleep on the job. Spurgeon and Moody were laymen, never ordained but bearing merely the title "Mr."

Then today there is radio evangelism and the tabernacles and youth movements and traveling evangelists and Bible conferences. Over the land there are prayer meetings and revivals and gatherings of Bible believers who are distressed over the times and are looking to heaven for a real awakening. I have just been reading an old, faded book about the great Welsh revival. Would that today there might come another such melting of our hearts in repentance and prayer and praise!

August 13, 1939

103

Indiana Reverie

This scribe is now in Berne, Indiana, preaching in the Mennonite church. Here is one of the most interesting communities in the land, a Swiss town set down in this beautiful farming country. The population is not much over two thousand and yet last Sunday morning there were around twelve hundred at the Mennonite church, and there are several other churches in town! It has been a long time since I have encountered such sturdy people and such a background of religious training. There is an atmosphere of old-world reverence as we assemble in the large and beautiful church to hear wonderful singing, for these people can really sing, and to hear the Word where it is still believed.

I am staying with an old-fashioned doctor who has practiced over forty years and still is going strong. I went with him on one of his rounds yesterday and had prayer in two homes at his request. He is the old type, sturdy, simple, and with a knowledge gained from experience that the experts have never reached.

If our country had more of such people as make up this community, we should be more hopeful. There is something strong, rugged, honest, law abiding, about such folk that reminds us of our forebears of other days. I have also found it in Swedish communities in Minnesota.

Each morning this week I am awakened by the strains of a gospel music broadcast by loud-speaker from the belfry of the church. The young people hold prayer meeting from 6:15 to 6:45 A.M. This morning I listened to the sweet comfort of the first verses of John 14, which could easily be heard all over town. Would it not be a blessed thing if one could so greet the day over America instead of being awakened by the raucous blasts of a radio swing orchestra?

Such a thing seems impossible to this poor, silly age, but we should all be far happier if we so lived. I find this a happy, thrifty community, and the smile of God seems to be upon it. Yesterday, visiting in one of the farm homes, I heard the housewife speak as naturally of the Lord's return as if she were talking about gardening. They have been brought up to believe God's Word and such a foundation is a base for real living.

Most of the trouble today lies at the door of the home. The family rarely can be assembled at one place and one time. The auto keeps them out, and when they are in the radio brings in the world, so there is little time for home fellowship. Everyone is up too late and must hustle to school and to work in the morning; at night there are the movies and a dozen other counterattractions so the family altar is a relic of the past. Mothers who used to teach their children the way of life now put them in movies or leave them with maids while they play bridge. It will soon be useless to sing "Tell Mother I'll Be There," for the modern mother does not seem to be going there.

It has been said that the trouble is not the hardness of the time but the softness of the people. Verily, we need a return to the things that cannot be shaken.

April 24, 1938

104

A New England Jaunt

I returned recently from a trip through New England. Now and then this scribe must invade a new portion of the U.S.A. It is a good investment, for no one can steal memories from you.

On the top of man's newest Babel, the Empire State Building, we looked down upon modern Babylon. We had been there before, but each time there is a new impression. Above, a dirigible went over. In the hazy distance we glimpsed the tower of Harry Emerson Fosdick's Riverside Church. From the harbor a liner put out to sea.

Through Connecticut and Rhode Island to Boston. The rocky New England coast. Portland, thence across by Sebago Lake to the White Mountains of New Hampshire.

Climbing Mount Washington, highest of them all, is a rare experience. Bright and sunny below, we found Labrador vegetation and a terrific wind on top that threatened to blow us away. And fog so heavy we must keep the lights on, and we missed the wonderful view for we seemed to stand upon a few feet of earth and look into a world of mist on every side.

On top we joined the "Club Among the Clouds." We meditated upon this and reflected that we belonged to a better club than that: a "Club Above the Clouds." Above the clouds of adversity and circumstance here on earth and above every cloud hereafter.

Coming down, we had a lesson in faith. I could see nothing, and the driver could see only a few feet ahead. At any point we might have swerved off into eternity. But I was depending on him. Is it not so with life? And how we fret and worry because we cannot see ahead when the driver has never lost a passenger!

Vermont is the fortieth state we have visited, and in some respects, I like it best. There is a calm simplicity and ruggedness about it, a pastoral charm to the quaint house-and-barn homes, a sturdiness that stands in sharp contrast to the artificiality of more modern communities. I should like to live in Vermont.

Across the Green Mountains, across Lake Champlain, and we are in the Adirondacks. Then to Albany and the Storm King route down the Hudson. Those who have been there know, and we cannot paint such beauty for eyes that have seen it not.

I spent several days in Washington again, as is my custom now and then. Tramping along Massachusetts Avenue to the Episcopal Cathedral to visit the tomb of Woodrow Wilson.

The lasting appeal of the Lincoln statue is the Memorial; the new Lincoln museum in the Ford Theater building; the room where Lincoln died. I sit in the grass at the Capitol while the band plays to a throng in the evening; many panhandlers on the streets; magnificent government buildings going up. Somehow there are so many solemn impressions that one gathers nowadays in such a center of the nation's life that it is good to steal away as I did down to Ocean View, Virginia. Yet commercialization has spoiled every beach resort for me. Sometimes one is fortunate enough to get away from it all far down the beach with the "sun and the sand and the wild uproar," as Emerson wrote.

And, best of all, it is to return to Pasquotank, where bull frogs jump from bank to bank.

September 18, 1932

105

Home Again

We are back in the hills again in old Catawba County, resting a little while before starting on a four-months' preaching trip. And where can one rest quite so well as among the familiar scenes of childhood?

I have been strolling down through the pasture and in the woods where we dreamed the long, long dreams of youth. It is springtime and never are the hills lovelier than now. Fleecy clouds go drifting overhead, the fog rises along the creeks, the mountains stand in the haze, wrapped in the early spring robes of tenderest green. The dogwood and honeysuckle are contesting for the honors of sweetest loveliness.

Bird lover that I have been, I find ample opportunity to refresh my acquaintance with the songsters that fill the woodlands with their morning music. The wood thrush, my favorite of them all, is ringing his bells and playing his flue as of old. The mockingbird is going over his varied repertoire. The vireos are conversing, sounding very much like one half of a telephone chat. The water thrush is ringing out his wild, challenging call. The prairie warbler is thrilling his little octaves and the pine warbler sounds his contented little chant. The ovenbird shouts his "preacher" song and the least flycatcher spills his rollicking melody. The yellowthroat, the hooded warbler, the crested flycatcher, and all the other host of my open woods concert are going strong. How easily one lets go the stress and strain and sinks into the sweet, old spirit of the hills!

What a contrast to come from a stroll and then listen to Hitler or the harrowing predictions of prophets scared over the war clouds! Why cannot this be a world of peace and why must men devour one another? Because sin abounds, and the human heart is deceitful and desperately wicked, and men will not come to Christ that they might have life. So, much as we would like to stay in the hills, we must be going to preach the gospel and labor while it is day, because the night cometh when no man can work.

It has been a joy to preach for several evenings in the old home church at Corinth. The neighbors whom we have known through the years come in from the farm labors and listen to the wandered returned. A blessed time we had, and there was a gracious response, for the coals of spiritual zeal still glow in many a heart. If we blow upon them, and men stir up the gift of God a bit, the flame will glow again.

Often we have thought that if this world can be as pretty as it now is, marred by sin, how lovely will it be when He whose it is shall come to reign! He is our hope, and the earnest expectations of the creature waits for the full manifestation of the sons of God. Even so, come, Lord Jesus!

May 7, 1939

106

Along the Canyon

One experiences a peculiar thrill when he draws near to a sight he has long desired to see. It was with expectant delight that I boarded the train at Williams, Arizona, to visit the Grand Canyon.

Now and then along the journey I would gaze across the sands hoping to catch a glimpse of the wonder I was riding to see. But the traveler gets no suggestion of it, and it is only when he has climbed the steps from the station up to El Tovar, the hotel on the Rim, that the natural masterpiece of all earthly wonders breaks into view before his awestruck gaze.

I know better than to try to describe it. If you have been there, you know, and if you have not, words cannot convey more than a pitiful suggestion of this gigantic miracle of the ages. Men have sought to trap its mysterious features by brush and camera and word picture; but before no other wonder of earth does a mortal feel quite so helpless to comprehend and transmit what eye hath seen and soul hath felt.

As with other things, greater than the Canyon itself is the atmosphere of it. One cannot express it secondhand, for as in relating a dream, the best part gets away. But in this hurrying, feverish age, what a changed perspective we might have if every harassed soul of us could spend a while now and then on the edge of this quietest spot in all creation and think a while upon the why and wherefore of life's little puzzle. Here one sits as though a lone survivor on the rim of a desolate and deserted world, chasms reaching far to the distant skyline and into which cities might be tossed like pebbles—a world of mystery slashed into gashes miles deep. How trifling our huge worries seem; how our fretful little concerns shrink away before this silent witness whose testimony the ages do not change!

Strolling along the border of this miracle of the Eternal, one feels as never elsewhere the weight of the Bible injunction, "Be still, and know that I am God." We have grown self-congratulatory over New York skyscrapers; a dose of the

Canyon ought to stop our chatter. There is scant time for meditation on Broadway; but in God's Arizona silence one can fade out of this world of time and sense back into the limitless ranges of His eternity.

Only those whose eyes look through His marvelous grace can rightly read His message anywhere. To admire God is not to know Him. But doubly beautiful to the soul who knows the Maker are the things that He has made. And one comes away at eventide from the Canyon, its castles and minarets and spires transformed into unutterable loveliness in the glow of sundown, thanking God that even more glorious than this sublimity is His love for poor, sick souls that seeks and saves and will not let us go.

September 27, 1936

PART 12

Scattered Reflections

107

This 'n' That

Once more the little plum bush is in blossom out by the old road. It is one of the advance notices of spring. There is a delicate fragrance about it that whets one's appetite for the sunny day ahead, as though in its tiny white blossoms it had caught and distilled the sweet, subtle spirit of April and May. There is something about these harbingers of spring that always touches pleasant chords in my soul. It cannot be set down in our clumsy words so I shall not try. But it does awaken each year the boy in me that refuses to grow up and sends me away to the woods and meadows saying to myself, "Ah, what do business and success and prosperity matter if one knows how to live understandingly in the world of bud and brook and birdsong!"

People who do not understand such things will wonder why I write such bunk. Those who do understand will wonder why I don't write more of it.

Jazz is not music—jazz is an excuse for not being able to make music.

Feathers do not make the bird. I have observed that some of the birds most brightly plumaged, like the bluejay, are the poorest singers, while others in modest colors, like the wood thrush, are most musical.

Here is a Bible verse some of us have forgotten: "He that will love life, and see good days, let him refrain his tongue from evil, and his lips that they speak no guile." Backbiting is the favorite indoor sport of too many church members. People who love to stir amongst rotten reports must enjoy the smell.

Jesus did not say "Shine your light" but "Let it shine." It will not be necessary to flare your goodness to attract attention. Some make a business of trying to be influential, but influence is a by-product, not a business. The fragrance of a flower is not its main business. To produce fruit, results, is your business; your fragrance, your influence, is incidental.

Speaking of business, what a difference there is between busyness men and businessmen! The former just do things; the latter get things done. Is your work a business or just a busyness?

My Bible says: "He that observeth the wind shall not sow; and he that regardeth the clouds shall not reap." Don't bother with the wind and clouds; stick to your farming. Spiritually speaking, don't bother with doubts, fears, appearances, uncertainties; live up to the best you know. Too many Christians watch the elements, looking for suitable intellectual states and pleasant emotional conditions, and there is no harvest. Ours is to trust and obey in season and out of season. There are no ideal farming years, but we usually have crops. Grow the best life you can with the soil you have and don't think too much about the weather.

March 16, 1930

108

The Country Store

The old-fashioned country store is a passing institution, rapidly being choked to death by the modern chain systems, which in all fields of activity are killing out independence and originality. Before they ultimately fade out, perhaps a brief eulogy would be fitting from one who often has stood behind the scales.

The country store nowadays is a place where people buy things on their credit when they are not able to pay cash at town. The storekeeper has the pleasure of booking customers until they find a few dollars; then he gets to watch them ride by, headed for his nearest competitor. Most of the articles he sells he makes a measly profit or even loses money on; if there is any profit in it, they buy it at town.

It is useless for him to stock up on anything to wear; people will pay a double price in the city for the same material to save the embarrassment of saying they bought it in the country. He tries to help his neighbor by crediting him and thereby loses his trade, for when the account reaches its limit the customer goes elsewhere with his cash. The rural merchant is an asset, for he saves his friends many a trip to town for little necessities they must have; they do him the return favor of going over to Main Street when there is heavy buying to be done.

If it were not for a few loyal customers with a heart, the country store would be as extinct as hoopskirts. As it is, there is no class more familiar with adversity than the rustic merchant with a salesman coming every hour and a set of books that a magician couldn't balance. Somewhere there ought to be a generous reward for country preachers, doctors and storekeepers. I imagine that when the final roundup comes, the last three to come in will be these ministers, merchants, and medicine men who have been out looking for those accounts that never came in.

If I wanted to find the ideal place to check up on a community's religion, I'd get behind the counter in a country store. You will discover wonderful things there. Some of the Amen

Corner Brigade at church are the last to square up for their groceries. There are deacons and elders and sometimes a parson who owe for the rations with which they started housekeeping.

When Zacchaeus was converted he squared up his past debts. One of the best ways to prove the sincerity of a man's religion is to watch what he does with his grocery accounts. Too many churches today are cursed with a front-seat hypocrite who sings and prays like a saint and owes everybody in the neighborhood—with no intention of paying them. If a man love not his brother whom he has seen, how can he love God whom he has not seen? And no man can love his brother and fail to treat him fairly in business. If you can not use your spiritual coinage in your community marketplace, they have no use for it in the vaults of heaven.

No name will show up well on God's great ledger that rates *bad* on your grocer's files. While paying your debts doesn't save you, you'll pay them because you're saved.

Don't snub your rural merchant. If he is dying out, at least try to make it painless.

November 23, 1930

251

109

Except Ye Be Childlike

Not long ago I loafed all morning in a small town, waiting for my "ship" to come along. On a grassy church lawn I "unlaxed" and watched the world go by.

There came along somewhere a dainty, light-haired, blue-eyed, little child just out to pass the time away. Together we sat through the sunny morning and became good comrades in that artless playfulness that our superficial modern sport tries so vainly to recover. Finally the little fellow must go, and as far as I could watch down the street, he turned every few seconds to wave a fresh good-bye.

That left me in the grass a little lonesome and "smitten with the plague of thought." The Master said, "Except ye be con-verted, and become as little children, ye shall not enter into the kingdom of heaven," and I do not wonder that He said that. How we do strain and pose to be impressive when the truest soul is most gently simple and childlike! When the Lord wanted a type for His disciples He set a little child in the midst of them. Some of us need to lay aside our weighty volumes and forsake our strenuous strivings to learn a lesson from the babies.

Truly, God's deepest secrets often miss the wise and prudent and are revealed unto babes. We say, "Children, be like your parents." Jesus said, "Parents, be like your children." We sometimes speak of old people as having reached their second childhood. No greater lesson can any mortal master than to learn how spiritually to be a child again. To reach in the realm of the soul that sweet simplicity, that utter trust, that freedom from grinding worry and care, that clear-eyed sincerity, that buoyant inner playfulness—to be in spirit what the baby is, naturally, is a triumph of first magnitude. We believers were meant to be like that anyway. It is our natural estate in Christ. Just as the old Adam nature starts out playful and gladsome, so the new nature we are born into in Jesus is also joyous and hilarious. The difference is that the natural child spirit tones down with the sobering of the years; but the eternal life we share with God grows more radiant as the life wears on, for while the outer man decays, the inner is renewed.

So, when my little playmate left me on that fair spring morning, I breathed a prayer within: "Lord, help me as I ramble through these earthly days to keep the heart of a child. Help me never to soil my soul with that sham hypocrisy that seeks to hide its spiritual hollowness with the mask of smartness. May I never get used to living but keep that sense of wonder and adventure that never lets life become commonplace and dull. Keep me clear and clear-eyed, unweighted with a guilty conscience. Let men call me impractical and strange. I crave not this snappy, modern efficiency which is only a cloak for a restless soul. Let me move through these years, a joyous person on this little speck of stardust, to whom a bird song, a blue sky, or a playing child means more than the blatant hilarities by which sin-sick moderns try vainly to pass the time."

Blessed are the children and the childlike, for theirs is the kingdom. And one day when the strange tangles of existence have all been straightened, we shall play in the gardens of His redeemed earth, which only the weak and gentle can inherit.

May 24, 1931

110

As a Little Child

A friend of mine said to me recently; "One thing about you I'm certain of. You'll never grow up; you'll always be just a kid."

I am sure that a psychiatrist, if he analyzed me and assorted my complexes and inhibitions in Greek-termed rows, would classify me as a grownup who refused to be his age. He might call me a case of arrested development. He might shake his head sadly and call me a lot of things.

I hope I never grow so mature and settled and established that I do not feel my heart turn over or want to click my heels in the air when on a sunny May morning I stroll along a pasture lane in the blossom-scented freshness, while the cardinal sings his matins and the wood thrush rings through the woodlands his sunrise chimes.

There are two kinds of folks I'm happy with: children and the childlike (all others are clowns). I like to lay aside the mask of our dignified masquerade and loaf along some crawfish creek with a bevy of stub-toed kids. There is a life for you! Or else, I like to chat with one of those rare souls who has returned in spirit to his second childhood and carries in his heart sweet, simple, perennial youth.

For what a strained and stilted pretense we wear our fool selves out keeping up! Sometimes I have sat with a man for an hour, both of us rigid in a labored pose trying to be impressive. Then one of us would drop a sly remark that would "let the cat out" and down would come our dignity in clattering ruins amid a gale of laughter. Then we could be human and friends.

And I recall that the greatest of all who have dwelt among us said, "Except ye be converted, and become as little children, ye shall not enter into the kingdom of heaven." I never heard a sermon from that verse, and if I did it likely would blur the real meaning with some colorless platitude. Should not a Christian always carry the carefree heart of a child? Does not he drink from God's fountain of eternal life and youth, and has not his Master bidden him not to worry and fear but to live in utter trust and happy abandon to the eternal Father? Where did we get that doleful funeral face—exactly the opposite of the shining countenance of His saints? We ought fairly to skip through life for all things are ours, and if we are in Him absolutely nothing need give us a mournful mien. We are the Father's true children amidst a prodigal race, and the grave is but the gateway to our true home beyond. We ought to be the happiest souls alive, for if we share His life we never grow old; the outer man decays but the inner is renewed day by day; we really should grow younger until the little clay house collapses and we go home. For we truly have that fabled fountain of youth: "Whosoever liveth and believeth in me shall never die."

So let me spend my days a grown-up "child" in a very mature and grim old world that frowns at the capers of a genuine and spontaneous spirit. I am not fretted with their petty bother about earth's trinkets and trifles, its success and its silver, its hollow thrills and theories. I am God's child in a world He meant for our playground, and one day I shall dwell in His redeemed creation, where even the leopard shall lie down with the lamb, the lion and calf together—"and a little child shall lead them."

April 23, 1933

111

Framing Our Faith

In this day when so much incense is being offered to the great god of system, when everything has been organized until all you hear is the creaking of machinery, I crave to vex the efficiency experts with the following rumination:

Bernard Shaw said: "Americans have the best filing systems in the world but no American can ever find a letter."

We practical Americans have arranged, classified, and catalogued everything from molecules to the millennium. In our mania for framing things we have forgotten that the best things of life cannot be caged, that life is unorganizable, and that when we build tabernacles to house our visions, we pretty soon have nothing but the tabernacles.

Especially is it true of religion. You cannot organize religion. The very minute you take an emotion and try to make it into an institution, you kill it. When will we ever learn that we cannot preserve, propagate, and perpetuate any truth by organizing a club in its honor with a moderator, a desk, a roll call, and a set of laws and by-laws?

You cannot institutionalize religion any more than courtship or poetry. When you try to frame faith, you have nothing left but the frame. Religion has never accomplished much save when it has managed to break through the creeds and forms and organizations that have been built around it. The very machinery with which we seek to propagate truth is usually the greatest barrier to its progress. We have labored for centuries perfecting our creeds and ceremonies and church paraphernalia, and after all our trouble, we never do any noticeable good until we manage to forget our catechisms and let our hearts outrun our heads.

For truth is not scattered by argument but by infection and contagion and influence. We have written libraries defending truth and explaining truth and propounding truth, and it has mostly been in vain. The Word must become flesh and dwell among us.

I am weary of committees and club meetings and church

conventions and sessions of the rabbis. I am fed up with campaigns and drives. I am nauseated with theological hairsplitting. I am disgusted with this orgy of competitive church building, each denomination trying to outdo the other with a representative church in our capital and everywhere else. It is born of the same secular, materialistic spirit as our overorganized, systemized, modern craze for worshiping the letter and forgetting the spirit.

We are getting nowhere by it for we are more interested in frameworks than in faith and works.

It is time for a new prophet to cry out: "Incense is an abomination unto me; the new moons and sabbaths, the calling of assemblies, I cannot away with; it is iniquity, even the solemn meeting. Your new moons and your appointed feasts my soul hateth!" Time to quit building scaffold for our beliefs; God wants some fruit out of His orchard.

December 4, 1927

112

From the Valley of the Shadow

A few days ago my father died. I have just come back, it seems, from the Valley of the Shadow in which I walked with him a ways to where we parted, and he went on upon that strange journey we all must go. By his bedside I watched the wonderful mystery by which the little spark called *life* fades out, and a pulsating human being becomes a few pounds of cold clay.

It was the first time within my knowledge that the Reaper had broken into our own immediate little circle. I had often wondered at a distance just how I might react to such a tragedy. I have discovered that the terrible thing we call *death* is not so hideous if we see it aright. Though of course I am immeasurably poorer for the loss, I am also far richer in spirit for the experience.

Like most other things it is not the actual truth about death that is so terrible as the great bugaboo we have built around it. Death the reality is simply that little step in the process of Nature by which a bit of life changes its form, laying aside one spent shell to assume another. There really is no death. Nothing dies. Forms change but life itself runs right along, picking up new manifestations and embodying itself in new shapes.

So I do not feel in this instance as if some fearful break had occurred in the order of things. The passing of my father is one tiny episode in a beautiful drama that seems often unintelligible to us, the spectators and actors, but which is quite full of meaning to the Great Producer. I accept the episode and leave the why and wherefore with the Master Dramatist.

But I would not have you think that I am only a cold philosophizer and nothing more to whom such an event supplies only a text for a newspaper article. There was and is a tenderest phase in this parting of a boy and his dad.

My father took me, as a tiny tot, to church every Sunday. It was rather burdensome to me sometimes, and the sermons went over my head, but the sense of reverence instilled by that routine has proven a mainstay many times since. Some of you dads, mulling over your Sunday cigar and too lazy to take your kids to some worshiping place, need not be surprised if they make sorry reports in the days to come.

Another memory lingers. I was always running around over the country preaching hither and yon. Every time the train pulled me back into Hickory or Newton, I looked for the welcome glimpse of Dad in his faded old suit, standing beside the little old Ford to greet me. It will seem strange to not see him so again. But in this sophisticated age I am still old-fashioned enough to believe that when the final lap of life's great trip is rounded and I pull into the Grand Central in some far finer land, the familiar face glorified and made radiant in the world where the Lamb is the Light shall greet me anew.

January 20, 1929

113

Is This the Whole Show?

A note in the papers: Two little children killed in their parents' automobile by an airplane that failed to take off.

A horrible tragedy that no pleasant platitudes can soften. And, what is worse, but one of hundreds of like gruesome calamities happening continually all over the world, crashing suddenly without warning and leaving behind no reason or explanation—just bitter and benumbing despair.

In the wake of such miseries, bursting hearts raise questions too painfully borne to be lightly regarded. Is there a God or only cold, inexorable, impersonal law? If there is a God, why does He send us little children to be brutally snatched away just when we love them most? Where is there any sense and reason in such whimsical turns of fate that preachers call *providence?*

Such aching hearts are not to be met with superficial rose-water, arm-chair theories framed by pious professors who have never known in personal experience that of which they speak. Here is no opportunity for shallow optimists and grinning Pollyannas who have not "been there."

We do not understand why such things happen. Nobody else does. It would take God Himself to unravel the intricate problem involved in the whole matter of trouble and suffering. Much of it does appear unreasonable and even heartless—a tangle no mind can straighten out.

But much of our mental misery over the subject is due to a partial survey. We view the matter as though this life were all there is to it, as though this world were the whole show. We think of death as ending everything in spite of our Easter declarations. We are looking at eternity but what we see is only that little section of eternity we are passing through here—for this life is but one little chapter of life itself. We can't get ourselves out of the habit of measuring the whole by one tiny part.

If this life were all then indeed would injustice seem to reign. But we neither start nor stop here. We began as a self-conscious personality when we were born but the various elements that make us up stretch back through all eternity.

We are part of eternity—and eternity yet to come. The death of two children viewed as an isolated incident may indeed from the temporal standpoint seem without meaning; but as a detail in the great design of eternity it takes on an entirely different light. Who knows what further plans God may have for those lives, what purpose He had in letting them live here awhile? Apart from the fact that such calamities have transformed lives of bereaved ones left behind and given them a new outlook, deeper sympathies, and keener anticipation for the life to come, may not the Eternal purpose be moving lives on to a greater career when we see nothing but wretched tragedy?

We see only one little chapter in the great story of the universe. We rashly judge infinity by the few unfinished sentences—incomplete at both ends—that we read here. Could we see from lofty eminence the whole drama of God from start to finish, the tiny little incident we called bitterest tragedy might bring a smile instead of a tear; sorrow might become gladness and pain only an incidental prelude to eternal joy.

February 9, 1930